MODERN
MUSTANGS

MODERN

MUSTANGS

TWENTY YEARS OF 5.0 MUSCLE

Jim Campisano

MetroBooks

MetroBooks

An Imprint of Friedman/Fairfax Publishers

©1999 by Michael Friedman Publishing Group, Inc.

Library of Congress Cataloging-in-Publication Data available upon request.

ISBN 1-56799-697-3

Editor: Ann Kirby

Art Director: Kevin Ullrich

Designer: Milagros Sensat

Photography Editor: Valerie E. Kennedy

Production Manager: Camille Lee

Color separations by Fine Arts Repro Houes Company Ltd.

Printed in China by Leefung Asco Printers Ltd.

10 9 8 7 6 5 4 3 2 1

For bulk purchases and special sales, please contact:

Friedman/Fairfax Publishers

Attention: Sales Department

15 West 26th Street

New York, NY 10010

212/685-6610 FAX 212/685-1307

Visit our website:

http://www.metrobooks.com

DEDICATION

This one's for my son, Sam, a chip off the old small-block, and my faithful dog, J.D. What can you say about the pooch who kept me company into the wee hours of the morning while I wrote this?

ACKNOWLEDGMENTS

First, I must thank Nathaniel Marunas of Friedman/Fairfax Publishers. In a world flooded with books about 1965–1973 Mustangs, he shared my belief that one dedicated to newer Mustangs could be successful. Without his efforts, *Modern Mustangs* would have probably remained an unfulfilled dream.

Special thanks to my friends and colleagues within the Mustang hobby who contributed to this work: T.S. (Tim) Boyd and John Clor, formerly of Ford's Special Vehicle Team; O. John Coletti of Ford Special Vehicle Engineering; Bernie Golick; Robert Lyons, founder and president of the SVT Cobra Owners Association; and SVO enthusiasts Lee Cleary and Ken Schultz, who graciously took the time to impart their knowledge of these special Mustangs and send me volumes of information about them.

Thanks also to Al Kirschenbaum, whose 1979–1993 V8 Mustang Reference Guide is the absolute last word on all things Fox-related, for selflessly sharing with harried magazine editors; my staff at *Muscle Mustangs & Fast Fords* magazine for making me look good all these years; Jim McCraw; Steve Saleen; Kim Seguin; Kenny Brown; Cari Southworth; Dario Orlando; Jerry Heasley; Tom Vogele and Craig Nickerson of McMullen Argus Publishing; and Sanford Block, curator of the ASC/McLaren Registry.

And thanks to the 100,000 or so readers of *Muscle Mustangs & Fast Fords* magazine—the most loyal, supportive audience a writer/editor could ever hope for.

CONTENTS

Introduction

Fabulous Fox Mustangs
Twenty Years of Power and Performance

For those who didn't live through the 1970s, it is hard to fathom just how awful cars had become during that decade. Bombarded by ever-increasing government regulations and constantly attacked by the insurance industry and environmental groups, the Big Three automakers were under siege. They responded by churning out some of the most forgettable, uninspired, and unreliable conveyances to ever turn a tire. The final kick came in the form of the Arab oil embargo of 1973. The American car-buying public—which for years had embraced Detroit's bigger, faster, thirstier offerings with what could almost be described as religious zeal—began looking to Japan and Europe for its transportation.

Not that these imported cars were much better; truth be told, at this point there wasn't much to recommend them other than that fact that they were smaller, and thus more fuel-efficient. The car-buying public, dazed by long lines at gas stations and stunned by prices that doubled seemingly overnight, traded in its fuel-guzzling luxury cars and overpowered muscle cars and buzzed back home in Datsuns, Toyotas, and Volkswagens.

These were truly the automotive dark ages. Gone were the Pontiac GTOs, the Cobra Jet Fords, and the Hemi Road Runners and Barracudas; these ground pounders were replaced by teeny, tiny imports with sewing machine–size engines. Perhaps no car better symbolized how the mighty had fallen than Ford's Mustang. Once the automotive embodiment of the swinging '60s, it had evolved (devolved?) into the Mustang II, a tepid machine based on the lowly Pinto econobox. Still reeling from the oil embargo, buyers snapped these up at first, only to realize very quickly that they'd been suckered. This wasn't a performance car—it was a joke.

That's what made the arrival of the 1979 Mustang so exciting. Based on the newly developed "Fox" chassis (which it shared with the previously introduced Ford Fairmont), it harbored new and innovative technology that, though not revolutionary, certainly offered a glim-

mer of optimism to traditional Mustang enthusiasts and to those longing for some of the driving fun that had been missing since the '60s. Turbocharged engines, sleek aerodynamics, and vastly improved handling signaled that maybe, just maybe, there was some hope for the '80s.

Who could have known then that twenty years later the Fox-based Mustang would not only still be in production, but would be a linchpin in a grand new era of high performance? The Fox Mustang endures, and it became one of the most revered automobiles of its time, creating a furor the likes of which hadn't been seen since the original Mustang's introduction in 1964.

It's an amazing story, and thankfully, it isn't over yet. As this is book is being written, Ford has just taken the wrapper off the 1999 Mustang, the first major revamping of the Fox-4 platform. The '99 has gotten a complete facelift and an improved suspension, and a 260-horsepower V8 will be standard in the GT. At the same time, engineers, designers, and marketing people are readying the Fox Mustang's replacement, which is expected to debut around the 2001 model year. It could be based on a totally new chassis, code name DEW-98. Others say it will spring from the proposed Fox-5 chassis, a furthur update of the venerable platform of 1978. More than likely, it will be the finest, most sophisticated ponycar yet.

Without a doubt, the new Mustang will owe a huge debt of gratitude to its forebear, the Fox Mustang, whose inherent goodness has allowed it to survive into the twenty-first century. Certain automobiles define specific eras: the Model T, the '32 Ford, the '55 Chevy, the '65 Mustang, and the '69 Camaro. The Fox Mustang has become the sporty car for the masses in the late 1990s, an icon for an entire generation of hot-rodders.

And while it isn't the perfect car, the Fox Mustang's popularity has lasted two decades and will have spanned two centuries by the time its run is over. We wonder: will anyone be writing a book about the 2001 Mustang twenty years after the fact? We'll see.

Opposite: In 1979, Mustang performance didn't get much better than the turbocharged 2.3L Cobra with the TRX tire/suspension package. Its four cylinder engine made 132 horsepower. **Above:** Twenty years later, the 4.6L SVT Cobra is Ford's peak performer. Its dual-overhead cam V8 makes 316 horsepower.

Chapter One

1979–1982

Here Come the Foxes

Anyone who remembers President Gerald Ford's WIN ("Whip Inflation Now") buttons, the Iranian hostage crisis, and discomania will tell you that the 1970s were more than just a little bizarre as far as decades go. Polyester leisure suits were high fashion, the world was running out of oil, and scientists said the next ice age was imminent. If you loved cars, things were every bit as strange. "Performance" meant obnoxious tape stripes, emasculated engines, oddball styling, and fake scoops and spoilers. It was grim.

By 1978, the lone survivors from the ranks of the 1960s muscle cars were the Chevrolet Corvette and Camaro Z/28 and the Pontiac Firebird Formula and Trans Am. But while they lived on in name, their once-throbbing powerful engines were no longer available, choked by emissions-control devices, and/or detuned to the point where they barely ran.

As for the fabled Ford Mustang, it was rechristened the Mustang II in 1974 after undergoing its first ground-up redesign. Many customers had complained that old Mustang had grown too large: with each successive restyling throughout the 1960s and early '70s, it swelled in size and weight to the point where calling it a ponycar was a bit of a misnomer. "Plowhorse" was more like it.

Ford responded with a major downsizing. The Mustang II was based on existing Pinto underpinnings, and that meant it shrunk from 189.5 inches (481.3cm) in overall length in 1973 to 175 inches (444.5cm) a year later—making it 6.6 inches (16.7cm) shorter than the original early 1965 Stang. The wheelbase was reduced from 109 to 96.2 inches (276.8 to 244.3cm).

The Mustang II was smaller and lighter than the car it replaced, but many key aspects of the first Stang's success were missing.

Reliability, for one. Handling, for another. Panache? Virtually none. As for performance, it was practically nonexistent. Originally, there were only two engines offered: a 2.3-liter overhead-cam (OHC) four-cylinder and a 2.8L V6. The idea of a Mustang without an optional V8 engine seemed unthinkable, but it was a reality. First-year sales were strong, no doubt buoyed by the frenzy to purchase fuel-efficient autos following the 1973 Arab oil embargo. And although the 302 V8 did return in 1975, sales of the Mustang II had already started skidding.

Then, also in 1975, the strangest thing happened. Consumers, seemingly having forgotten how fuel scarcity and high prices had held them hostage just a short while before, started flocking to Pontiac dealers to purchase gas-guzzling Trans Ams and Formulas. And they did so in record numbers. Once the supply and price of fuel stabilized, people couldn't wait to get back behind the wheels of these 400- and 455-cubic-inch ersatz supercars.

Ford countered in 1976 with the Shelby Mustang–inspired Cobra II, but it was a sheep in wolves' clothing. While the Mustang II Cobra II's twice-stripes and snake emblems were reminiscent of Ford's mid-'60s maulers, the car's acceleration was anything but. Even by late-'70s standards, the Cobra II was a stone.

HELP IS ON THE WAY

In the fall of 1977, Detroit rolled out its latest offerings. The hoopla from Ford surrounded the introduction of a new family of midsize cars, starting with the Ford Fairmont and Mercury Zephyr. On the drawing board since the early '70s, they were going to be America's first line of defense against the ever-increasing onslaught of imported machinery. They replaced the dreaded Ford Grenada and its equally forgettable cousin, the Mercury Monarch, and were touted as the family cars of the

future. Based on what was known inside Ford as the Fox platform or chassis, both cars were light in weight, roomy, fuel-efficient, and sturdy—if less than exciting. (Ford had been in the habit at the time of internally naming its platforms after animals, hence the Fox name; there was also the Panther line, among others.)

Then–Ford boss Lee Iacocca had given the green light to the Fox cars way back in 1974, and when they arrived as 1978 models, they were generally well received by both the automotive media and the buying public. Styling could charitably be described as conservative, though some might call it stodgy. It wasn't, however, offensive to the eyes, as were many Chrysler and General Motors offerings of the day. And the Fox cars looked positively beautiful next to the creatures being sold at American Motors dealerships.

Despite the boxy styling of both the Fairmont and the Zephyr, it was under the skin where they earned praise. A modified MacPherson strut front suspension and rack-and-pinion steering gave them handling that was a

Preceding pages: The '82 Mustang GT funneled its exhaust into a single tailpipe with twin tips. Exterior color choices on the GT were limited to red, black, or silver. This example has the optional TRX metric tires and wheels; 14-inch (35.5cm) tires were standard on the GT. **Above:** One of the highlights of the lost Mustang years (1974–78) was the Mustang II Cobra II. Drawing inspiration from the first Shelby Mustangs, it kept Ford's performance image alive—even if it was on life support. **Opposite:** The date was July 31, 1978; the place was Ford's Rouge Assembly plant in Dearborn, Michigan. One of the first Fox Mustangs, a coupe, has its body lowered over the rear axle assembly.

quantum leap ahead of almost any sedan previously built in America, but without a harsh ride.

Motor Trend magazine described the Zephyr as "one of the most impressive surprises of 1978," while *Car and Driver* noted that it had "the agility and handling feel of an import."

Part of the Fox sedans' agility was due to their reduced weight, a necessary part of the plan to increase fuel economy. Ford liberally used plastics, aluminum, high-strength low-alloy steels, and thinner glass (among other things) to pare weight to a minimum. And it worked: even a 302-equipped Fairmont would be hard-pressed to tip the scales at more than 3,000 pounds (1,362kg). That was 600 to 1,500 pounds (272.4 to 681kg) less than the typical family car of the day, and the reduction improved every aspect of the Fox twins' performance—handling, braking, acceleration, and, most important to the parent company, fuel economy.

Car Craft magazine was the only publication that saw the potential for all-out performance from these otherwise plain-Jane offerings. In its June 1978 issue, its staff was more than impressed with the Fairmont's 3,000-pound (1,362kg) curb weight and its potential for outrageous power-to-weight ratios. The Fairmont tested for that story had but 145 horsepower and an automatic transmission, but it could smoke its right rear tire all day long and run with other, more "sporty" cars.

One thing that went unnoticed was that the Fox-chassis cars were not just large on the inside. While Grandma and Grandpa could appreciate the voluminous interiors, their hot-rodding grandkids would one day learn to appreciate the cavernous engine bays.

REBIRTH OF A LEGEND

At one point in the mid-1970s, the market for high-performance vehicles hit an almost inconceivable low. Chevrolet killed the Z/28 after the '74 model year, and the General was actually considering scrapping the Camaro and Firebird lines altogether.

Then, inexplicably, Firebirds started selling again. Fueled by the high-speed antics of Burt Reynolds and

WHOSA FOX, WHATSA FOX?

Fox means more than just Mustangs. So, what exactly are the cars that comprise the Fox family of Fords? From 1978 through 1988, Ford based a number of sedans, wagons, ponycars, and sport coupes on the incredibly adaptable Fox platform.

1978–1983	Ford Fairmont, Fairmont Futura, Fairmont wagon; Mercury Zephyr, Zephyr Z-7, Zephyr wagon
1979–1986	Mercury Capri
1979–1993	Ford Mustang
1980–1988	Ford Thunderbird and Mercury Cougar
1981–1982	Ford Granada and Mercury Monarch
1983–1986	Ford LTD and Mercury Marquis (models with 105.5-inch [268cm] wheelbase only; larger LTD Crown Victorias and Grand Marquis models were not Fox chassis–based)
1983–1986	Lincoln Continental
1983–1992	Lincoln Mark VII

Note: The 1994–present Mustang is based on a revised Fox platform that Ford calls the Fox-4 (the "4" stands for 1994, the model year it was introduced). Thus, it is still regarded as a Fox Mustang.

Jackie Gleason in the movie *Smokey and the Bandit*, Firebird sales reached unprecedented levels. At the same time, the Mustang II's reputation was at its nadir. It was laid to rest in 1978.

The good news was that unlike the vast majority of sporty cars and muscle cars from the '60s, the Mustang would soldier on. In 1979, it was reborn as a Fox-bodied vehicle, and for the first time since 1973, it had a ponycar stablemate that shared its underpinnings. That car was the Mercury Capri.

To keep costs down, Mustangs had always been based on an existing model. The first generation was built on the Falcon chassis, the second on the ill-fated Pinto. For round three, Ford chose the Fairmont's Fox underpinnings, and while this wasn't the sexiest foundation, it was leaps and bounds ahead of the Falcon and Pinto. Its advanced engineering allowed Ford to build sturdy, very light, efficient cars for the next two decades.

The '80s were a time of still more governmental regulations dictating crashworthiness and increased fuel economy. If nothing else, the Fox chassis proved its adaptability.

Up front, the Mustang utilized a modified MacPherson strut arrangement with the coil springs located low on the vertical struts. The rear featured four trailing arms and a live axle, and there was a coil spring on either side. Rack-and-pinion steering was standard (a carryover from the Mustang II) and radial tires were optional. Even in base trim, the result was a nimble, fun car that could be tossed around corners. For a buying public weaned on wallowing 4,500-pound (2,043kg) Thunderbirds and ill-handling beasts like the Grenada, the Fox Mustang and Capri were eye-opening.

An optional handling suspension was available for $33 and provided firmer shocks and struts, springs, bushings, and a rear sway bar (14-inch [35.5cm] radial tires were mandatory). It provided improved cornering, but you could still take your Mustang to another level. For true enthusiasts, Ford offered the TRX tire/wheel/suspension option. It was engineered around four Michelin TRX metric radial tires (190/65R390) and comprised of special-rate springs, revised shock and strut valving, and front and rear sway bars. The end result was the best-handling Mustang yet.

"In the handling department, at least, the TRX package does for the Mustang/Capri what the Trans Am option does for the Firebird," noted the August 1978 issue of *Hot Rod* magazine. "The steering and brakes—both borrowed from the Fairmont/Zephyr—are the best yet for a Mustang. The power-assisted, variable ratio, rack-and-pinion steering provides maximum effort and minimum ratio at the dead center position; as the steering wheel is rotated, the effort decreases and the ratio increases."

On the downside, the metric radials were inordinately expensive to replace, in part because of their odd sizing (15.3 inches [38.8cm] in diameter). Many owners upgraded to more traditional 15-inch (38.1cm) rims and

tires at replacement time and ditched the three-spoke alloys and Michelin tires that came with the TRX package.

BEAUTY IS SKIN DEEP

Ford had taken plenty of heat over the styling of the Mustang II (it was far too Pinto-esque) and took great pains to assure that the new Stang made an aesthetic impact. Styling was under the direction of Jack Telnack, whose talents would one day put him in charge of design for the entire Ford Motor Company. He was credited with penning the fastback roofline of the 1965 Mustang and would later help revolutionize the auto industry in the 1980s with the swoopy, aerodynamic shape of the first Ford Taurus.

Increasing pressure on the Big Three in the form of increased fuel economy standards meant that the new Mustang would need as slippery a shape as possible. Telnack's team, which included Fritz Mayhew, David Rees, and Gary Haas, knew that by reducing aerodynamic drag, they could increase miles per gallon. On the other hand, these men understood that the sporty

Below: Mercury's "Sexy European," the Capri, became an American citizen in 1979. It abandoned its German roots and was built alongside the Mustang on the Fox platform. **Following page:** Those looking for more comfort opted for the Mustang Ghia, this one a 1980 model. Base price was $5,935 for the 3-door version.

Fox twins would have to retain traditional ponycar themes, such as the long-hood/short-deck look that defined the genre. Ultimately, models of the new Mustang and Capri would spend 136 hours testing in the wind tunnel at the University of Maryland to help smooth the shape. It worked. The two-door coupe had a coefficient of drag (CD) of .44, and the three-door hatchback an even more impressive .42.

Helping achieve these wind-cheating numbers on the Mustang was a laid-back, egg crate–style grille, a significant departure from Ford's traditional upright front fasciae. (The Capri would get the traditional vertical nose and pay a slight aero penalty for it. Available only as a three-door, its CD was .44—certainly very respectable and good enough to allow Mercury to brag in its advertising that the Capri had a lower CD than the new Corvette.) The cowl was raised an inch (2.5cm) higher on both cars, giving their front ends a sleeker, more rakish appearance.

That the new Mustang was almost devoid of chrome could be attributed to both changing market tastes and Telnack's time spent in Europe as Ford's vice president of design. A wide rubber molding wrapped around the entire vehicle. For the first time since 1969 (and only the second time ever for the Mustang), Ford equipped its pony with four headlights—this time small rectangular units. A steeply raked (for the time) windshield enhanced the car's sporty lines and also aided aero.

In the rear, the traditional three-bar vertical taillamps were replaced with a six-bar vertical motif (five red bars and one white for the backup lights). On the whole, the new Fox Mustang bore little, if any, resemblance to the ponies that came before it. The Mustang II embraced many of the styling cues of its ancestors—three-bar taillights, an open-mouthed grille with single headlights, the C-shaped side indentation, and so on. Obviously, Ford chose to break completely from the past with the '79 Stang. Only the roofline on the two-door coupe (also known as a notchback) could be considered a carryover, and even that was a bit of a stretch.

Where the Mustang and the Capri had once been two distinctly different automobiles (from two separate continents, no less), there was no mistaking that now they were based on the same chassis. The Capri's nose and bulging fenders differentiated it from the Mustang's sleek, sloping proboscis and traditional flared wheel wells, and there was no notch for Capri lovers, but now both cars were built on the same assembly lines. It is interesting that the styling didn't seem all that bold back then. In a world where lower, wider, and shorter define sports car styling, the Fox Mustang was narrow at the shoulders and appeared a bit tall. But it endured with only slight tweaking for fifteen years; the basic shape remained the same.

INSIDE OUT

The European influence was quite evident in the Mustang's interior. While the Fairmont's dash was employed, there were complete gauges available located directly in front of the driver (speedometer, 8000-rpm tachometer, amps, water temperature, oil pressure, and fuel level). A leather three-spoke steering wheel was offered, and column-mounted stalks controlled such things as the windshield wipers and washers, horn, turn signals, and headlight dimmer. This doesn't seem like such a big deal today, but at the time it was a fairly radical departure on a domestic automobile.

As was typical, the base Mustang interior was sporty, yet spartan. It was up to the buyer to outfit his pony with as many optional goodies as he could afford. Among the options were a tilt steering wheel, leather seating surfaces, a four-way manually adjustable driver's seat, and an AM/FM radio with 8-track tape player. The interior option that got the most ink in the press was the available $140 console. It came with a digital clock that displayed the time and date, plus it had a graphic display of the car with warning lights for burned-out bulbs, low fuel, and low windshield washer level.

Thanks to an increase in exterior dimensions, interior volume was up from the Mustang II as well. Yet overall vehicle weight was down by a couple of hundred pounds. All hatchback models came with fold-down rear seats, which in the down position gave the sportier appearance of a two-seater.

A more important aspect of this feature, however, was that the it gave the Mustang the most stowage room in ponycar history. With the hatch open and the seats down, you could easily load large objects in the back, making the Mustang ideal for active young Americans. When the car began making significant horsepower in the early 1980s, racers learned that the hatchback models could swallow tools, a jack, racing tires, and most everything else needed for an outing at the track.

PERFORMANCE

While the Fox Mustang didn't have enough firepower to make people forget about the Cobra Jets and Bosses of the old days, it did promise more pep than the old Mustang II.

There were five choices among four engines offered during the 1979 model year. Standard in the Mustang was the old 2.3L overhead-cam engine. With a two-barrel carburetor, it made a meager 88 horsepower. A German-built 2.8L V6 was the next step up with 109 horsepower, but because of a shortage of these engines, an awful American-made inline six replaced it partway through the model year (it made just 85 hp from 200 cubic inches).

For the first time in years, Mustang lovers looking for extra performance had a choice of two engines, each very different from the other. There was a turbo-charged version of the 2.3L four-cylinder, or the old standby 302, now known in the metric '70s as the 5.0L. (Actually, this was a misnomer. The 302 displaces only 4.9 liters, but it was given the 5.0 name because at the time Ford also had a 300-cubic-inch six-cylinder truck engine. In order to avoid confusion by having two 4.9L engines, and perhaps at the same time in an effort to make the engine sound larger than it actually was—Pontiac was selling 6.6-liter Trans Ams and Formulas, after all—the 302 was christened the 5.0.)

The four-banger was equipped with a Garrett TO3 turbocharger that made a maximum of 6 pounds of boost (psi). It differed little from the base Mustang engine, but the TO3 "hair dryer" increased horsepower to 132 at 5400 rpm.

To monitor the turbocharger, two lights on the dash indicated whether you were inducing boost, and there were audible warnings for overboost situations and excessive oil temperature.

Mechanically, the 5-liter V8 was basically a carry-over from 1978. There were, however, a few differ-ences. A single-belt (serpentine) drive belt system worked the engine accessories, which added some horsepower. It weighed slightly less, thanks to an aluminum water pump and intake manifold. These engines used a two-barrel carburetor (for 140 horsepower at 3600 rpm) in every state except California, where emissions regulations dictated that the Mustangs be fitted with a variable venturi (VV) carburetor.

RECOIL—THE COBRA SAGA

Back in 1976, America had begun rekindling its love affair with high-performance cars. To counter the popularity of the Pontiac Trans Am and Formula models, Ford dug into its glorious racing past and came up with the Mustang II Cobra II, a car whose styling themes echoed those of the championship-winning Shelby GT350 Mustangs built by Carroll Shelby.

Even though the Cobra IIs were rather limp-wristed performers, Ford discovered there were plenty of people who fondly recalled those earlier Mustang Cobras. Sales of the Cobra II were brisk indeed, and when the Fox Mustang was introduced in the fall of '78, the top-of-the-line performer was the Cobra (gone were the Roman numerals).

Available only in three-door hatchback form, the Fox Cobra came standard with a "high-output" engine, the turbocharged 2.3L four. For better acceleration, a 3.45:1 rear axle ratio was standard, and the excellent TRX handling/suspension package and four-speed overdrive transmission were part of the deal as well.

Instead of fake wood, a black "engine turned dash appliqué" was affixed to the instrument panel. The Mustang's optional gauge cluster was standard and carried the boost lights and audible warn-ings if you stayed with the turbo four. A faux forward-facing hood scoop aided with the visuals, as did a host of "Cobra" insignia inside and out. (A massive Cobra graphic for the hood was optional, a nod to the Trans Am's "screaming chicken.")

Window frames and moldings were blacked out, as was the paint below the wide body molding. Aluminum rear brake drums and front discs were standard as well.

"Ford Mustang Cobra. Sporty appearance is only half of its good news." That's how Ford trum-peted the arrival of the new snake in its sales brochures. "For some cars that call themselves 'sporty,' appearance is everything. Literally. But fear not, for the '79 Cobra is here and better days are ahead. Days of driving fun that maybe even you thought were beyond your dreams."

Sure, it was a lot of hype for a car that couldn't be ordered with more than 140 horsepower. Even if it wasn't the fastest new car on the road, it was at the very least a capable handler that was fun to drive and easy on the eyes.

From an enthusiast's standpoint, the turbo cars handled better thanks to their lighter weight and better weight distribution. Acceleration was another matter. Although horsepower was similar between the two engines, the V8 made far more torque and was able to get the jump on the four.

In an effort to make the cars seem quicker than they were (and since the national speed limit was federally mandated at 55 miles per hour [88.4kph]), Ford no longer quoted 0-to-60-mph (96.5kph) times. For the turbo Mustang, it rated a 0-to-55-mph (88.4kph) elapsed time of just over 8 seconds. *Car and Driver* still used the more accepted 0-to-60-mph (96.5kph) time, and a 5.0 car it tested was capable of achieving that

velocity in 8.3 seconds. *Car Craft* clicked off a quarter-mile (402.3m) time of 16.49 seconds at 84 mph, which, while not earth-shattering, was significantly quicker than the 1978 Mustang II, which would take about 17 seconds flat to accomplish the task.

The four-cylinder turbo was standard in the Cobra model and was available as an option in any other Mustang for $542. The V8 was a no-cost option in the Cobra, but would tack on an additional $514 to the price of any other Stang. Both were backed by the Borg-Warner single-rail overdrive (SROD) manual transmission as standard equipment. The 5.0, though, could be had with an automatic, which helped give it an advantage in the sales department.

The 1980 Cobra had the look of speed, but it lacked the muscle to back up its brash appearance. Cobra package cost $1,482 (three-door only), plus $88 if you wanted the hood decal.

LEADER OF THE PACK:
THE 1979 MUSTANG PACE CAR

Ford held nothing back when it came time to promote its new Mustang. It realized that the car had tremendous potential and would exploit it however possible. To this end, Ford negotiated to have the Mustang named the official pace car of the '79 Indianapolis 500. Ford was cognizant of the fact that this was more than a race; it was a living, breathing spectacle witnessed live by hundreds of thousands of people, with many millions more watching on television. There is also the blizzard of media attention bestowed upon the pace car honoree. That translates into sales of both the standard model and the obligatory "pace car replica."

Ford didn't disappoint the Mustang faithful. It had been fifteen years since that day in 1964 when a Mustang convertible first paced the big race, and the car Ford built to do the job in 1979 was more than up to the task. A special Jack Roush–built 302 made in the neighborhood of 265 horsepower, and with wild paint, graphics, and bodywork, it stood apart from the base Mustang. Naturally, Ford offered a "limited" number of replicas (without the good engine, unfortunately) to be sold in dealerships around the country.

Visually, the Mustang Pace Car benefited from a raised cowl-induction-style hood; nonstandard-issue pewter paint with a unique graphics package; a revised, blacked-out grille with horizontal bars; and a bold front air dam with integral fog lights. At the rear was a Pace Car–only hatch-mounted spoiler. Highlighting the black striping on the hood (the car was also black from the molding down) were red and orange stripes. Another set of red and orange stripes started at the front by the side marker lights and ran down the fenders and doors before extending up and over the roof.

All replicas featured the TRX suspension, and power came from either the 5-liter V8 or the 2.3L turbo. Inside, the Pace Cars used the same Recaro sport seats as the actual race pacers—the first time these high-dollar buckets were available in a production Mustang. There was a simulated engine–turned–instrument panel appliqué similar to the one used on the Cobra. Other optional features that were standard on the Pace Cars were the leather-wrapped steering wheel, deluxe seat belts, and the console with graphic warning-display module and digital clock.

The engine in the actual Pace Car featured a host of high-performance goodies that enabled it to stay ahead of the field. The heavy-duty blueprinted block held a Boss 302 forged steel crankshaft and connecting rods, TRW pistons, specially prepared 351 Windsor cylinder heads with 1.84-inch (4.6cm) intake valves and 1.54-inch (3.9cm) exhaust valves, a Boss 302 cam, a dual-plane aluminum intake manifold, and a 600-cfm Holley four-barrel carburetor.

Although the exact number is still not known today, more than eleven thousand Pace Car Mustangs were built and sold in 1979, making it one of the most successful Pace Car replicas ever, regardless of manufacturer.

INTO THE 1980S

Though somewhat forgotten twenty years after the fact, the '79 Mustang was very successful. Sales were up drastically, from 192,410 to 369,936. Everything seemed to be on the upswing. For performance enthusiasts, however, things took a drastic turn for the worse with the introduction of the 1980 models. Gone from the options list was the 5-liter V8, a casualty of tightening emissions and fuel economy standards. It was replaced by an anemic 255-cubic-inch V8, which was a downsized 302 (a 3.68-inch bore vs. a 4.00-inch bore) with more restrictive cylinder heads and a choked intake manifold. Horsepower from the 4.2-liter engine was an agonizing 118 at an uninspired 3800 rpm. To add insult to injury, it could only be ordered with an automatic transmission.

This made the 2.3L turbo the top gun—for a while, anyway. After the 1980 model year, it was discontinued due to reliability problems. This was mostly a carry-over year with very few changes. The Recaro seats from the '79 Pace Car became a $531 option on any Stang. Plus, the Pace Car's air dam, rear spoiler, and hood became standard on the Cobra. Halogen headlights provided better visibility at night, but they were hardly the stuff performance dreams were made of.

Like Ronald Reagan's presidency, the '80s started off slow for the Mustang. With the 2.3L turbo temporarily relegated to history, 1981 was not a memorable year. Engine choices were the 2.3L naturally aspirated four-cylinder, an inline 200-cubic-inch six more suitable for farm equipment than a ponycar (94 horses), and the 4.2 V8, now "boasting" 115 horsepower (120 in California, thanks to its VV carb). Had Dr. Jack Kevorkian been assisting suicides then, the Mustang would have been an excellent candidate.

Power windows made their return in 1981, as did the Traction-Lok differential. There was little else to get excited about other than the introduction of the T-top removable roof-panel option. The actual '79 Mustang Pace Car had this feature, but production cars could be ordered only with a pop-up sunroof (actually called the flip-up, open-air roof). Now, for $916, your ponycar

Below and left: The Mustang that saw actual duty pacing the Indy 500 sported a Jack Roush–built 302 that used a heavily fortified bottom end and modified 351 cylinder heads. Those sold to the general public got the far less interesting 140-horsepower 302 seen here.

could be fitted with the removable glass panels. They proved to be very popular—keep in mind the reintroduction of the Mustang convertible was still two years down the road—but they did compromise the car's structural integrity and were prone to leaks, squeaks, and rattles.

The end of the year saw Ford discontinue the Cobra name. It would not reappear until 1993, and when it did it would be on a car far more deserving of the appellation.

THE BOSS IS BACK

With Chevrolet and Pontiac poised to introduce all-new Camaros and Firebirds in 1982, Ford had to do something to keep the Mustang attractive to prospective

customers. What it did was reintroduce the fabled Mustang GT, a name not used since 1969, with a breathed-up on version of the 5-liter V8. Called the 5.0 H.O. (High Output), it delivered 157 horsepower to the ground and 240 pounds-feet of torque, enough to easily smoke the pretty new Camaro/Firebird twins from General Motors.

The print ads screamed, "The Boss Is Back." Ford was returning to the high-performance game, and it did not do so timidly.

"The word is out on the street. It's Mustang GT. Sharp, street smart, and powerful...It's one of the meanest-looking Mustangs we've ever built. But that's our opinion," the ads bragged.

In a *Motor Trend* shootout, the Mustang whipped the Camaro in a March 1982 acceleration test, which showed the Mustang dust the Camaro from 0 to 60 mph (96.5kph)—7.78 vs. 8.58—and to the end of the quarter mile (402.3m)—16.26/83.70 vs. 16.67/81.00.

What made the GT tick? Its 5.0 engine had a large Holley two-barrel carburetor, a high-performance camshaft, and a double-roller timing chain. The power was sent via a four-speed transmission to a 3.08:1 Traction-Lok rear end—both mandatory. Like the Cobra and Pace Car before it, the GT wore a large front air dam with Marchal fog lights, revised grille, and rear spoiler. Instead of the raised cowl hood, a fake forward-facing scoop was fitted. The only available colors were

Opposite: If Ford built an '82 Mustang convertible for production, this is what it would look like. It's attractive, but the ragtop wouldn't reappear until 1983.

Below: Ford reintroduced the Mustang GT in 1982 with a 5-liter H.O. engine. Its 157-horsepower engine was a fine performer in its day, but would soon be eclipsed by the '83 GT's 175 horsepower.

red, black, and metallic silver, which could be had with either red or black interior.

Underneath, the handling suspension with 14-inch (35.5cm) wheels and tires was also mandatory, as were power brakes and power steering. The handling suspension came with a traction bar to help eliminate wheel hop. The TRX tire-and-suspension setup was an extra $111 on the GT.

So impressive was the Mustang GT's performance that the California Highway Patrol snapped up four

hundred of them for high-speed-pursuit duty, beginning a twelve-year love affair between the cops and Special Service Package (SSP) ponies. (A total of thirty-five states and more than one hundred sheriffs' departments ordered these Mustangs before the SSP was discontinued following the '93 model year.)

A new era of high performance—the modern muscle car era—was dawning, and the Mustang would be at its forefront. It went from the doghouse to the penthouse almost overnight, and the best was yet to come.

2 1983-1986
Fox Tales

 No doubt Ford had a winner on its hands with the 1982 Mustang GT. Sales of this model were very strong; it had garnered the lion's share of rave reviews in the press and helped divert the media's attention from its sleek new ponycar competitors at General Motors.

The reality was, however, that the Blue Oval gang was just getting started with the Mustang GT. For 1983, a substantially more powerful 5.0 was unveiled in a face-lifted Fox body. To make matters even more interesting, a Turbo GT became available midway through the year replete with a revised version of the 2.3L four-cylinder power plant.

These performance models helped revitalize interest in the Mustang, even in the face of stiffer competition from domestic rivals like the Camaro and Firebird and from increasingly popular imports such as the Toyota Celica. Even with the 5.0 engine, the Mustang's sales fell by more than fifty thousand units in 1982 to 130,418 (a sagging economy also held it back).

For enthusiasts, 1983 would turn out to be a banner year for the ponycar—if not from a sales standpoint (they actually fell again, to 120,873, making it the Mustang's worst year ever to that point), then from the total number of significant new features and models that debuted.

MORE OATS IN THE FEEDBAG

With fuel prices and availability once again stabilized after another shortage early in the decade, America's lust for faster, more exciting cars kept growing. Ford didn't disappoint. It endowed the Mustang with its first four-barrel carburetor since 1973. Mounted on an aluminum intake manifold and fed cold air by a large, dual-snorkel air cleaner was a 600-cfm Holley/Motorcraft carburetor; horsepower

jumped from 157 to 175. Torque was rated at 245 pounds-feet at a low 2400 rpm.

Except for these parts, the 5.0 engine itself was basically a carryover from '82. The restrictive exhaust manifolds, single catalytic converter, and muffler were all off the '82 GT. You could only get a manual transmission with the 5-liter H.O., but the four-speed SROD transmission would bite the dust a few months into the model year, replaced with a version of the Borg-Warner T-5 five-speed overdrive gearbox. The T-5, originally offered in four-cylinder Mustangs, was a much-improved transmission over the SROD and was strengthened for use behind the V8. Improved gear ratios made it more compatible with the power band of the 5.0. Unlike the SROD, which was overdriven in fourth

gear, the T-5 had a more usable 1:1 ratio, with fifth gear (overdrive) being 0.725:1 for improved fuel economy.

For quick acceleration, the 7.5-inch (19cm) rear end was equipped with 3.27:1 Traction-Lok gears (it was the only available setup for '83). And accelerate these cars did. *Mustangs & Fords* magazine out of California tested an '83 with the SROD transmission and blazed the quarter mile (402.3m) in less than 15 seconds (14.89 to be precise) at 92.03 mph (148kph). *Popular Hot Rodding* magazine ran a best of 15.01 at 93.34 mph (150.1kph) with a T-5 version.

Preceding pages: Ford celebrated the 20th anniversary of the Mustang in 1984 with an anniversary edition. All were based on the GT, were painted oxford white with canyon red interiors, and had red tape stripes running along the rockers with "GT350" lettering. **Above:** The Fox Mustang got its first face-lift in 1983, and thanks to a four-barrel carb and new intake manifold, it could back up its racy looks with tire-smoking performance.

As with the '82 GT, the handling suspension with 14-inch (35.5cm) wheels and tires was standard. The upgraded TRX package was still popular, but the size of the metric Michelin tires increased from P190/65R390 to 220/55R390. To better control the newfound power, the size of the rear sway bar was increased, the shocks were recalibrated for quicker rebound, and the steering was quickened by some 20 percent.

Yes, the '83 GT was still a bit on the raw side, but consider this: it could accelerate as well as a new Corvette, but it cost half as much. Top speed for an '83 GT hatchback was close to 130 mph (209.1kph), some 14 mph (22.5kph) less than the Vette.

The '83 Mustang GT was more than a match for the '83 Camaro Z/28, if not in all-out acceleration then in bang-for-the-buck excitement. *Car and Driver* did a shootout with a 5.0 H.O.-equipped Camaro in its June 1983 issue, and although the Camaro was quicker to 60 mph (96.5kph) as well as in the quarter mile

(402.3m), the magazine had encouraging words for all Ford fanatics: "In sum, the Mustang builds up to its limits very quickly and in a fashion the citizen driver can use to excellent advantage."

It closed by saying, "If you like low-speed stunt driving accompanied by clouds of tire smoke, the Mustang GT gets it." And you could get one for just over $10,000—about $3,000 less than the Camaro.

In other midyear news, Ford brought back the turbocharged 2.3L engine, this time with a whole host of upgrades to make it more reliable and powerful. Lifted from the new 1983 Thunderbird Turbo Coupe, the 2.3 now had Bosch multiport electronic fuel injection, a reworked turbo that delivered boost quicker, a lowered compression ratio, and forged aluminum pistons, among other tricks.

Below and inset: For 1984, Ford offered an automatic transmission on the GT, but the only engine it backed up was the less-potent CFI 5.0 (inset photo). Though down just 10 horsepower on paper, it couldn't match the five-speed/four-barrel 5.0 performancewise.

FORCE-FEEDING AN ISSUE:
FORD'S TURBO MUSTANGS

It could have been the right car for the right time. The turbocharged four-cylinder Mustang, first introduced as standard equipment in the '79 Cobra, made decent power and offered good fuel economy, and its light weight helped keep unwanted tonnage off the Mustang's nose, thus aiding in handling. Eventually, reliability issues, inexpensive fuel, and the blessed neck-snapping acceleration that can come only from an American-made V8 doomed this engine.

For a long while, though, small force-fed engines like the 2.3 turbo appeared to be the wave of the future. The combined efforts of the OPEC oil cartel and the petroleum industry seemed to be dictating that America's long-standing love affair with large internal combustion devices was doomed. By 1973, fuel was expensive and sometimes difficult to locate. That meant a 460-cubic-inch V8, with its attendant 8- to 10-mile-per-gallon (12.8 to 16km per 3.7L) fuel economy, wasn't the wisest choice.

Of course, Americans hadn't given up their love of high-performance vehicles entirely. The question was, how could Detroit give them the power they craved (and had come to expect) without sacrificing emissions, fuel economy, and reliability?

For answers, the Big Three turned their attention to power adders, specifically the turbocharger. Oldsmobile was the first domestic manufacturer to offer one of these exhaust-driven units in a production car, the 1962 Jetfire sport coupe. To increase the output of the car's 215-cubic-inch V8, a turbocharger was fitted and the result was an engine that produced 1 horsepower per cubic inch, plus 315 pounds-feet of torque.

How? Inside the turbo housing is a turbine, which is spun by exhaust gases. Once the turbine starts spinning, it forces compressed air back into the intake system. This air, when combined with the proper amount of fuel and spark, can increase horsepower by 100 percent or more. Among the benefits of this was that there was little impact on fuel economy—during normal driving, a turbo motor would consume no more fuel than a nonturbocharged engine.

In the mid-1970s, Porsche used the turbocharger to made its 930 the fastest production car in the world. Buick began offering turbocharged six-cylinder Regals and LeSabres in 1978, and Ford debuted the 2.3L turbo in '79. In the Mustang, the turbo helped boost power from 88 hp to 132, or just about as much as the 302.

A Garrett AiResearch TO3 model turbo with a built-in wastegate was used (the wastegate started bleeding off boost at 5 psi and everything over 6). It fed a two-barrel Holley carburetor mounted on an aluminum intake manifold. The engine's electronic ignition was designed to retard the timing under boost to keep the engine from experiencing engine-damaging detonation (a.k.a. pinging).

To handle the rigors of turbocharging, which can be hard on internal engine components, the 2.3 received improved rod and main bearings, TRW forged pistons with special rings, and an upgraded oiling system. The cylinder head was fitted with intake and exhaust valves capable of dealing with the higher temperatures created by the turbo. The head was sealed to the engine with a solid-steel-core gasket. Increased cooling capacity staved off overheating, and a 3.45:1 rear axle ratio was employed for quicker acceleration—about 16.7 seconds in the quarter mile (402.3m) at 81 mph (130.3kph).

When reliability problems caused Ford to shelve the 2.3L turbo after less than two years of production, the Mustang was left without a single high-output engine until the 5.0 reappeared in the '82 GT. Ford wasn't finished

Ford reintroduced the turbocharged 2.3L four-cylinder engine in 1983. The Turbo GT now produced 145 horsepower, but couldn't match the performance or refinement of the less expensive (by $265) 5.0 GT. The turbo 2.3 went away for good in the GT the following year.

with four-cylinder "hair dryer" engines yet, though. The Turbo GT turned up as a midyear option in 1983, and the powerful Mustang SVO appeared a year later.

Thanks to Bosch electronic fuel injection, the 1983 2.3 produced 145 horsepower at 4600 rpm and 180 pounds-feet of torque at 3600. The engine featured other improvements and changes to enhance its reliability and performance. The compression ratio was lowered to 8.00:1 (from 9.3:1). Air conditioning was not available, which aided acceleration, as did the revised ratios in the T-5 transmission (first gear was an unbelievably low 4.03:1).

The Turbo GT engine was the first Mustang to use Ford's EEC-IV engine processor. This computer controlled all the engine's functions. It would later be fitted to the 5-liter engine with wonderful results.

Because of its performance, the four-barrel-equipped 5.0 overshadowed the Turbo GT, and fewer than one thousand of the latter were sold. In 1984, the option would prove more popular (3,798 sold), but the success of the 5-liter GT and the introduction of the radical Mustang SVO (also with a turbocharged four-cylinder engine, albeit a more potent version) doomed the four-pot GT. It would disappear after 1984.

Above: The script on the air cleaner lid said it all for Ford fans. The GT became a serious sports machine with this engine, which lasted in carbureted form through the end of 1985.

LET THE SUNSHINE IN

As wonderful as this newfound acceleration was, equally important was the fact that 1983 was the year Ford would bring back the Mustang convertible. It was resurrected after a ten-year absence, and 23,438 sun worshipers plunked down their money for wind-in-your-face thrills. To many, this made the Mustang lineup complete. For others, it was the only model worth having—regardless of the engine choice.

Against all odds, the convertible was making a comeback across the United States. Lee Iacocca, now the head man at Chrysler Corporation, took a gamble in 1982 and launched the Chrysler LeBaron convertible. Though based on the economy K-car, the LeBaron was an instant success. Soon, other convertibles appeared in the ChryCo camp, and it would not be long before other manufacturers followed suit.

Ford unleashed the Mustang droptop in November 1982, and it quickly established itself as the best-selling

convertible in America. The cars themselves were assembled on the regular Mustang line and then sent to Cars & Concepts in Brighton, Michigan, where they were finished (since 1981, all Stangs have been built in Dearborn, Michigan; previous Fox Mustangs had been built in Dearborn and in San Jose, California). All convertible Mustangs came standard with a power top and a glass rear window. To cope with the loss of structural integrity inherent to all open cars, a host of chassis braces was installed. While somewhat effective, the convertible Fox Mustangs typically loosened up with age and were prone to rattles.

Initially, the stylish ragtops were available only in upscale GLX trim with the 3.8L V6 engine standard. Naturally, the 5.0 V8 was available and the GT package was eventually offered late in the model year.

In the styling department, all Mustangs received a nose job. The front fascia revise was said to aid aerodynamics while at the same time keeping the body looking fresh. The GT's fake hood scoop was turned around, with the still-nonfunctional opening now facing the driver. Out back, the taillights were changed as well. Gone was the vertical motif; in its place was a horizontal style that made the car appear a bit wider from behind. The result was a handsome automobile that appeared somewhat sleeker than its predecessor.

Inside, the instrument lighting was changed to red, for both clarity and dramatic purposes.

1984— ORWELL WAS WRONG

Mechanically, Mustangs in general underwent little change for 1984; mostly it was a case of revising little things here and there and reshuffling the model lineup. The soon-to-be-legendary (though not until 1987) LX model designation appeared on sedan, hatchback, and convertible models as an uplevel trim package.

Still, there was some very significant news. You could finally order a 5-liter Mustang with an automatic transmission—Ford's automatic overdrive, or AOD for short—but if you did, your car would be equipped with throttle body fuel injection rather than the Holley four-barrel carburetor. The EEC-IV engine control processor now joined the 5-liter ranks as the management unit for all cars equipped with central fuel injection, as this setup was called. It was rated at 165 horsepower, which was only 10 less than the H.O. version, but it was substantially slower, in part due to the automatic transmission.

The transmission itself would develop a reputation over the years as a hindrance when it came to high performance. It was never really intended to work in such an environment. As a trans-about-town it was fine, providing smooth shifts and decent reliability. When it came to hardcore use, such as street/strip performance, it was somewhat fragile and inefficient, eating up about 30 to

40 horsepower compared to the T-5 (itself proving to be somewhat fragile under extreme conditions).

Mustang GT models got a revised front air dam with integral fog lights midway through the model year. Convertibles were available as both GT and LX models.

Two totally new high-performance Mustangs were offered during the year, the first with much fanfare. Both, however, became parts of Fox Mustang legend and lore. They emphasized handling, braking, and sophistication rather than all-out brute force. The first was the Mustang SVO, which debuted in the fall of 1984. This car (detailed in chapter three) basically was a fuel-injected, turbocharged, intercooled four-cylinder steed with a completely revamped interior and suspension. It was

aimed at the BMW/import crowd and was the first vehicle produced by Ford's Special Vehicle Operations skunkworks.

The Saleen Mustang was the other variant, a fully certified, legal-in-fifty-states automobile. And though only three Saleen Mustangs were built and sold that year, they paved the way for thousands more that would follow right up to this day. Built by Saleen Autosport in California, the cars featured heavily modified suspension systems designed for optimum road holding and, ultimately, racing.

There was also a third new pony package, the 1984½ 20th Anniversary Limited Edition Mustangs, cars that today are surrounded by some confusion. They were built to commemorate April 17, 1964, the day when the original ponycar went on sale. All were built as GT models and were painted oxford white with red GT350 tape stripes along the rockers and doors. The stripes and GT350 designation, of course, recalled the Shelby Mustangs of the mid-'60s. Another nostalgic touch was the running-horse emblem placed on the front fender between the wheel and the door. It was identical to the emblem found on 1965 Mustangs.

The interior of these limited-edition Stangs was canyon red and came with a version of the SVO's sport seats, as well as that model's three-spoke steering wheel. The passenger-side dash featured a commemorative badge, as well as a plaque with the car's anniversary serial number (this latter badge had to be specially ordered by the owner and was shipped to the dealer after a registration form was sent to Ford).

Under the hood, buyers had their choice of the 5-liter V8 or the Turbo GT four-cylinder engine. An even hotter 5.0 was scheduled to be introduced, but valve train and piston problems put the project on hold temporarily. The TRX wheel/tire/suspension package was offered but the handling suspension with 14-inch (35.5cm) tires was standard. By the end of the model year, 5,260 20th Anniversary Limited Edition Mustangs were produced.

Total Mustang sales were on the rebound. After a bleak 1983, Ford sold 141,480 ponycars, including 4,508 of the very expensive SVO versions.

GT VS. SVO: WHO'S THE BOSS?

With the SVO, Ford introduced the most expensive Mustang to date. Even in the swinging, supply-side '80s, $15,585 was a lot of cash to shell out for a car in its fifth model year, especially when you could purchase a GT for $9,774 (base price).

On the other hand, the SVO, with its fuel-injected, intercooled, turbocharged engine, proper Lear Siegler sport seats, Hurst shifter, and revised suspension (complete with 16-inch [40.6cm] Goodyear NCT tires), offered a lot of car for the dough.

Under the magnifying glass, the two cars looked like a good match, performancewise. The GT produced 175 horsepower at 4200 rpm and 245 pounds-feet of torque at 2400 (obviously, we are referring to five-speed versions, not the lower-output CFI/automatic-transmission cars); the SVO's hyper four-banger cranked out 175 horses at 4400 rpm and 210 pounds-feet of torque at 3000. The reality was that the GT's prodigious torque got the Mustang moving quicker, and even though it weighed a few pounds more, the GT could cover the quarter mile (402.3m) faster than the SVO. *Motor Trend* put an SVO through its paces and came up with a 0-to-60-mph (96.5kph) time of 8.12 seconds and a standard quarter mile (402.3m) in 16.08 at 86 mph (138.3kph).

When it came time for the road to turn, however, the SVO held a huge advantage, owing to its better balance, lighter weight, more fully developed suspension, and 16-inch (40.6cm) tires, which were worlds better than the Michelin TRXs.

Purists liked the SVO more, but hardcore Mustang fanatics voted with their wallets. Neck-snapping acceleration for thousands of dollars less was too good a deal for the masses to resist, and the GT outsold the SVO by almost 8.5:1 (38,194 vs. 4,508).

BETTER LATE THAN NEVER

Back in its October 1983 issue, *Motor Trend* magazine wrote in its Mustang SVO test about the new 5-liter V8 that would have "more than 200 horsepower" for 1984. Unfortunately, that prediction was a year off, much to the dismay of '84 Mustang lovers. On the other hand, it did become the standard internal combustion device in the GT in 1985. Also new for 1985 was a revamped front end that some said looked like a raccoon due to the mask-like blackout trim around the headlight buckets.

This would be the last year for a carbureted V8 Mustang, and with a little help from Ford, it went out with quite a bang. Output was now 210 ponies at 4400 rpm and 270 pounds-feet of torque. The 35-horsepower improvement was the result of steel tube "shorty" headers, which replaced the restrictive cast-iron manifolds, plus a true dual-exhaust system aft of the catalytic converter, a more radical camshaft (now with roller lifters), and more aggressive jetting in the secondaries of the carb.

Those who insisted on an automatic tranny continued to be saddled with the weaker CFI 5.0, though it was upgraded to 180 horsepower early in the model year, thanks mostly to the use of the H.O.'s tube headers and twice-pipes. (These shorty headers worked extremely well for factory pieces and were an integral part of the Mustang's performance until 1996, when Ford introduced a completely different "modular" 4.6L V8 into the Mustang.)

Not wanting to let the SVO fall too far behind, the folks at Special Vehicle Operations tweaked their turbocharged terror midyear and managed to coax an additional 30 horsepower out of the little engine that could. Boost was increased to 15 psi, larger fuel injectors were fitted, the intake manifold and camshaft were revised, and the exhaust was opened up a bit.

At the same time, the 1984 SVO was given new flush headlights, which gave the front end a sleeker and more integrated look. Goodyear Eagle tires replaced the NCTs, and stiffer shocks and a quicker-

ratio steering box were installed. Better still, the base price dipped to a low $14,806. The result was the best SVO yet.

With all this power going around, it spelled doom for the Turbo GT Mustang. Those looking for cheap speed could turn to the 5.0 GT or 5.0 coupe, while people interested in a high-tech turbo car could opt for the upscale SVO. The Turbo GT was not brought back after the 1984 model year.

Climbing behind the wheel of a 5-liter Mustang was quite an experience. Not since the heyday of the Boss 351 fourteen years earlier had there been such a thrilling engine sitting between the Mustang's fenders. The Fox chassis provided a lightweight foundation and the 5.0 produced gobs of torque, even at low engine speeds. Revving the engine and dumping the clutch produced clouds of acrid tire smoke and a howl of protest from the Goodyear rubber as it clawed the pavement for traction. Banging gears hadn't been this much fun in a long time.

"There isn't the slightest hint of the European influences that seem to characterize Ford's most recent efforts," according to *Car Craft* magazine in its August 1985 road test. "Rather, Ford's new steed is a no-nonsense, straight to the floorboard, good ol' American muscle car, complete with a torquey four-barrel carbureted V8, heavy duty drivetrain, and lots of snappy acceleration."

While the basic Fox Mustang was getting a bit long in the tooth to some (slicker, more aerodynamic shapes were being introduced all the time, and the Stang's narrow, upright design contrasted with its competitors' longer, lower, wider stance), there was no denying the basic wholesomeness of the package. The 5.0 was cheap, easy to work on, and extremely reliable. No wonder, then, that sales surged forward another 10 percent, to 151,514.

More than just the front fascia and engine were the recipient of changes. Gone was the TRX wheel/tire/suspension package. Goodyear "gatorback" tires (225/60VR15s) were at all four corners, now mounted on Ford's ten-hole (or "phone dial") alloy wheels. The Quadra-Shock rear suspension, which used four shock

absorbers to aid traction, was standard on all V8 Mustangs (coupe, convertible, and hatchback). This arrangement used two vertical shock absorbers and two horizontally opposed smaller shocks to put the ever-increasing horsepower to the ground. It worked well enough to eliminate the need for the "slapper bars" that were employed on earlier Foxes. (The Quadra-Shock setup had actually shown up on some late-'84 GTs and on all '84 SVO Mustangs.)

There were other suspension changes as well. The standard GT suspension (known as the Sport Handling Suspension when ordered on LX 5.0s) featured, among other things, completely different spring rates, larger sway bars, Tokico gas-filled shocks and struts, and quicker-ratio power steering. Previously, the TRX package used linear-rate springs—410 pounds (186.1kg) front, 175 pounds (79.4kg) rear—as did the handling suspension,

Opposite: Mustangs got another face-lift in 1985. The GT got blacked-out headlights, which became known as "raccoon eyes" to enthusiasts. **Above:** Hardcore enthusiasts in 1985 opted for the new higher-output (210-horsepower) 5.0 in the lightweight two-door coupe body.

although the rears were a bit softer. To aid handling and control, Ford used variable-rate springs all around, which in theory allow the spring rates to stiffen under load for better grip and stability.

The new wheels measured 15 by 7 inches (38.1 by 17.7cm) and were standard on the GT and eventually on 5.0 LXs as well. Because these were "regular" 15-inch (38.1cm) wheels, Mustang owners weren't forced to shop at Michelin dealers for new tires in an expensive, odd size, which could be especially problematic if you suffered a blowout in the middle of nowhere and needed a replacement quickly. First seen commercially on the 1984 Corvette, the Goodyears performed very well in the wet, which isn't surprising considering that they were descended from Formula 1 rain tires. (Though some sources reported problems in wet weather conditions, this had more to do with the Mustang's poor weight distribution than the tires.) They had a uni-directional tread pattern, which meant they had to be mounted facing a certain direction.

Upgrades to the interior included the '84½ anniversary model's cloth articulated sport seats (they were available in leather on LX and GT convertibles), a full-length console, better door panels and carpeting, plus more standard features. All V8 models got the SVO's excellent three-spoke leather steering wheel.

As noted earlier, the '85 Mustang benefited from a face-lift. Some magazines felt that it more closely resembled the SVO model, but that view is not shared here. The wraparound body molding was new as well, and that did echo the treatment on the SVO.

The 1985 Mustang did represent the end of an era. Word filtered out through the press that this would be the last carbureted V8 Mustang. For 1986, Ford was converting all the 5-liters—including the venerable four-barrel H.O.—to electronic fuel injection, a move many scribes felt would end hot-rodding as the world knew it. They encouraged readers to buy the '85 because, after that, the engine would be an unknown quantity. "As the carburetor disappears, so does the induction system as an area of backyard modification," predicted *Car Craft*. "The Boss may be the last Ford that is compatible with the idea of home mechanics. That is unless you have a master's degree in computer technology and electronic engineering."

INJECTION IS NICE

Ford did endow the Mustang with fuel injection for 1986, and it turned out to be a mixed blessing at first. Horsepower slipped to 200, but torque increased by 15, to 285 pounds-feet. All V8 Mustangs, whether T-5 manual- or AOD automatic-equipped, received the same engine for the first time since the GT's resurrection. Performance was every bit as good as, if not better than, that in '85. Though it was later learned that the car's cylinder heads were fairly restrictive (they were used on the Mustang for only that year), the engine's robust torque helped it record 0-to-60-mph (96.5kph) and quarter-mile (402.3m) times that were near equal to any American car short of a Corvette.

Below: The Fox Mustang received its second major face-lift in 1985, and the GT was bolder than ever. This iteration lasted only two model years. One of the few ways to tell an '86 from an '85 is the presence of the government-mandated center high-mounted stop light (CHMSL) in the rear. Sales for '86 were the highest since 1980, nearly 225,000.

MERCURY CAPRI: FAREWELL TO A FOX

The Mustang SVO wasn't the only Fox-chassied ponycar to bite the dust in 1986. The decision was made to pull the plug on the Mustang's Mercury stablemate, the Capri. Despite strong sales at first, the Capri never garnered the same kind of "must-have" reputation the Mustang did. Part of the blame could probably be placed on Lincoln Mercury dealers. Busy selling options-laden land yachts to the over-sixty crowd, they had little time or patience for a sporty model. Then again, young people in the '80s were more apt to shop at import stores for Hondas, Nissans, or Toyotas. During the "new wave" era, walking into a Lincoln Mercury dealership was akin to buying Pat Boone records.

Unlike the Mustang, the Capri was available in only one body style, the three-door hatchback. Its grille was more formal—bolt upright instead of laid back—but it had wider, bulging fenders that gave it a racier appearance than its Ford cousin. Buoyed by positive press and backed with decent advertising support, the Capri sold 90,850 units its first year out of the gate. But it hit the skids the very next year; only 62,592 left the showrooms in 1980.

Not even the high-output four-barrel 5.0 helped. The Capri RS was the top-of-the-line performance model and it had all the V8 Mustang's performance goodies, plus a rather attractive "bubbleback" rear window that distinguished it further from its Ford cousin. The turbocharged 2.3L V8 from the Mustang was available in the Turbo RS model. Still, sales stalled at 22,708 in '83.

There were some rather interesting Capri models. Besides the RS, there was the Black Magic Capri from 1981 to 1983, which was black with gold pinstriping and trim. *The Standard Catalog of American Cars, 1976–1986* states that there was a Black Magic Capri available that was actually white with gold accents, but this author has never come across one. For 1983, however, there was a companion model painted red, which was called the Crimson Cat. It shared the Black Magic Capri's gold accents as well as its two-tone interior. There was also an ASC/McLaren two-seat convertible, which will be dealt with in more detail later in this book.

By the time the plug was pulled in '86, annual sales were at 12,647, making the car little more than a novelty. On a positive note, more than 300,000 Fox-bodied Capris were built in eight years and they are often overlooked by enthusiasts. That means you can have Mustang-like style and performance for a fraction of the cost.

carburetor, but thanks in part to the adaptive nature of the EEC-IV processor, hot-rodding was about to enter a new golden age. It would take a couple of years for enthusiasts to sort out Ford's EFI setup, but once they did, they found out it was actually quite user-friendly. And for a generation weaned on computers, electronic games, and the like, the fuelie 5.0 with its attendant hardware wasn't too difficult to understand.

Thanks to the newfound power, Ford finally saw fit to install a stronger rear end in the Mustang. The 8.8-inch (22.3cm) rear replaced the 7.5-inch (19cm) differential that had been in the Fox car since its debut. The 8.8-inch (22.3cm) unit had seen duty in Ford's smaller trucks (such as the Ranger), and although it wasn't as bulletproof as the company's legendary 9-inch (22.8cm) rear, it was lighter and more than up to the task at hand. A set of 2.73 gears was standard on five-speed cars, and 3.08s were available as an option; automatics came one way, with 3.27:1 gears.

With GT and 5-liter LX sales soaring and gasoline cheap and plentiful, there was little interest in the more costly Mustang SVO. It had very good handling and decent (if not peaky) power, yet its high cost was hard to justify. Sales of the little buzz bomb were never great and it simply outlived its usefulness. Ford pulled the plug on it after the '86 model year.

That was about the only down note, however. Mustang sales in general exploded, topping out at 224,410—the first time they had exceeded 200,000 since 1980. America was crazy about fast cars again, and the Mustang had virtues that made it irresistible to a large number of people. Ultimately, it was just a lot of fun. Buyers had their choice of a V8, a pair of four cylinders, or a V6 engine, and automatic or manual transmission. There were three different body styles to choose from: sedan (coupe), hatchback, and convertible, and you could get a flip-open roof on the coupe or hatchback, or even T-tops on the three-door models. The list of options seemed endless; it was like the '60s all over again. You could order your Mustang tailor-made just for you. It could be cute, sexy, or muscle-bound; mean, economical, or luxurious.

How many other cars could do that?

Helping offset the asthmatic cylinder heads was an above-average exhaust system. The shorty headers breathed into a genuine dual-exhaust system for the first time. There were two catalytic converters for each side and a balance/crossover tube (called an H-pipe), which added a bit of torque and quieted the system slightly.

The induction system consisted of a two-piece intake manifold (with upper and lower portions), a 58mm throttle body, and eight 19-pound-per-hour fuel injectors. The brain of the system was Ford's EEC-IV computer. What the enthusiast press didn't realize at the time was that not only wasn't performance going to die with the

3

MUSTANG SVO
Ford's Sophisticated Fox

America's automotive tastes changed in the late 1970s and early 1980s. While many were turning to Japan for cheap, economical transportation, those with more money turned their eyes to Europe for sophistication and luxury. Brands like Audi and BMW, which had previously filled a relatively insignificant niche in the marketplace, were suddenly very much in style and, by the early '80s, the vehicles of choice for yuppies. The first wave of baby boomers had money to spend and they weren't about to drop it at Cadillac and Lincoln Mercury dealerships.

This generation had grown up on muscle cars and small imports like the Volkswagen Beetle. It put handling and driving excitement—traits that were difficult to find in American cars of the day—above a pillowy ride and pure luxury. The sports sedans, as they were called, were being snapped up in increasing numbers, and cars like the 3-series BMW and Audi 5000 were the hot ticket for those on the way up. Traditional American personal cars like the Mercury Cougar and Oldsmobile Cutlass were going out of fashion as fast as white patent leather shoes.

Ford countered this primarily German invasion with a multi-pronged attack. It recreated the Thunderbird and Mercury Cougar, relaunching them in 1983 on the Fox platform with more sporting intentions than either car had exhibited in more than two decades. The Thunderbird Turbo Coupe and the similarly equipped Cougar XR-7 garnered excellent reviews and were quite successful in luring buyers into their showrooms. Both were available with the turbocharged 2.3L four-cylinder engine and five-speed transmission, a TRX wheel/tire combo, and fine creature comforts in a driver-oriented cockpit.

Ford also created the Merkur division for LM dealers. It consisted of two Euro Fords revamped for American roads, a three-door turbo coupe called the XR4Ti, and a four-door sedan called the Scorpio.

create limited-production vehicles like the one that bore its name. One print ad defined the car and the people behind it. It was as much a mission statement as it was a tool to lure potential customers.

These are the men
This is the machine
These are the men of Ford Motor Company's Special Vehicle Operations. They are men more concerned about 0–50 than 9-to-5. Men who care more about getting through a curve than getting through the day. With that attitude, they created the machine...

The ad proudly described the SVO Mustang's numerous high-performance features, the likes of which either hadn't been offered before in an American car or hadn't been seen on a Ford in years—items like a turbocharged, intercooled overhead-cam four-cylinder engine, a Hurst-shifted five-speed gearbox, and adjustable Koni gas shocks and struts.

When the men of SVO were finished with the Mustang, there was little about it that didn't bear their fingerprints. The only interior color was charcoal, and the instrument panel was redone to match. The dash housed a complete set of gauges: oil pressure, water temperature, fuel level, and turbo boost (0 to 18 psi). There was also a tachometer and a rather unusual speedometer. Though the numerals stopped at 85 mph (136.7kph)—as required by a preposterous federal law—the markings continued up to 140 mph (225.2kph).

To ensure a proper driving environment, the pedals were repositioned for easier heel-and-toe driving, and a dead pedal for the left foot was added. The seats, the finest ever offered in a Mustang, were multiadjustable units from Lear Siegler. Available in cloth or leather, they had pump-up supports so that they could be tailored for a variety of drivers. A heavily padded, leather three-spoke steering wheel with a tilt feature was standard. There was even a "premium/regular" cockpit-mounted fuel control switch, which allowed the driver to reprogram the engine control computer to allow for varying grades of gasoline.

Preceding pages: Ford got sophisticated in 1984 with the SVO Mustang. It was available only in silver, charcoal, black, or red. **Above:** With a $16,000 price tag, the SVO appealed to a more upscale buyer. It was priced about $6,000 more than the 5.0 GT. **Opposite:** A bi-plane rear spoiler and unique taillights differentiated the SVO from more common Mustangs, as did flush 16-inch (40.6cm) wheels.

Ford's other significant new vehicle was the 1984 Mustang SVO. With this car, Ford attempted to give the emperor new clothes. It took the preeminent American ponycar and, through the use of technology, ergonomics, clear thinking, and restyling, assembled a potent performance car that was still all Mustang but with a decidedly European flair.

In 1981, Ford assembled the Special Vehicle Operations team, a group of about twenty-eight men, and part of their job was to overhaul the Mustang so thoroughly that it would lure buyers from BMW showrooms. At the head of this consortium, which comprised some of Ford's most talented people, was director Michael Kranefuss. Ford SVO was going to supervise the company's return to motorsports, be responsible for creating a performance parts program, and, of course,

In December 1983, a number of options became standard, including power windows and locks, AM/FM stereo with premium sound, and interval windshield wipers. This is how the vast majority of cars were built for the entire three-year production history, so it is possible to find some unusually equipped early SVOs. A popular option on all Mustangs in '84 was the flip-up sunroof.

The exterior was the most obvious area of change. The front end was completely different from that of the standard Mustang and had what Ford described as a "grille-less" design. Large, rectangular headlights flanked a slit-like opening, and a wide, rubber body molding encircled the body. Integrated fog lights were housed in the valance under the bumper. An offset, functional hood scoop fed cool air to the engine's air-to-air intercooler. Flush 16- by 7-inch (40.6 by 17.7cm) wheels with low-profile Goodyear NCT tires (from Germany) filled the wheel wells. Fairings just ahead of the rear tires were installed to direct air around the massive rubber, thus improving aerodynamics.

"External body changes on the SVO set the car apart from other Mustangs (and everything else), but the cosmetic enhancement has a clearly functional air," said *Motor Trend* magazine in its first road test in October 1983. "Though the basic Mustang contours are looking more boxy and upright every year, the SVO people have managed to give them a contemporary look."

Motor Trend praised the SVO's "strikingly revised" nose but correctly noted that the car would look a lot better once fitted with the just-legalized flush-fitting headlight lenses (which would arrive in mid-1985).

Another aero aid that attracted plenty of attention was a biplane rear spoiler. It was said to eliminate lift and create downforce at high speeds, though it was even more successful as a conversation piece. A similar-looking spoiler had been used earlier in Europe on Ford's Sierra XR4i and again when the car was imported to America as a Merkur. Other changes included different taillights with amber turn signals and unique sail panels aft of the rear quarter windows. Color choices were limited in '84 to black, silver, charcoal, and canyon red.

While the interior and exterior refinements were wonderful, it was the suspension and engine upgrades that completed the package, and thus made the SVO truly special. At the core of the suspension upgrades were the 16-inch (40.6cm) wheels (with five lug nuts instead of the standard Mustang's and GT's four), 225/50VR16 tires, and adjustable Koni shocks and struts. Rarely seen on production automobiles because of their high cost, the Konis were symbolic of just how serious the SVO people were about making this Mustang handle.

Spring rates and bushings were also changed, and sway bars were fitted front and rear. It certainly didn't hurt handling that the SVO carried 150 fewer pounds (68.1kg) on the front end than the Mustang GT. This helped make it a much more neutral package.

As the Mustang SVO was an all-around road car and not just a straightline bandit, Ford saw fit for the first time to equip it with four-wheel disc brakes (11-inch [27.9cm] ventilated units up front, 11.6-inch [29.4cm] ventilated pieces in the rear). In the *Motor Trend* test, they hauled the Mustang SVO to a stop from 60 mph (96.5kph) in a very efficient 155 feet (47.2m).

Most interesting was the engine. The Mustang SVO got the same basic power plant as the force-fed 2.3L engine in the Turbo GT, but it featured a substantial increase in horsepower—30—thanks in large part to its air-to-air intercooler. An intercooler drops the air intake charge considerably, making it denser (able to carry more oxygen). In simplistic terms, the more oxygen and fuel you can jam into a cylinder, the more power it will generate when greeted with the proper amount of spark.

Also working in the engine's favor was its multipoint fuel injection, a more aggressive spark/fuel map in its electronic engine processor (compared with the 2.3 turbo engine from the Mustang and T-Bird/Cougar twins). The turbocharger featured an electronic wastegate to bleed off pressure from the turbo, thus allowing the car to be tuned for more performance (14 pounds of boost max).

The end result was a 140-cubic-inch engine that made 175 horsepower—the same output as the GT's 5.0 V8—at 4500 rpm and 210 pounds-feet of torque at 3000 rpm. *Motor Trend* reported acceleration times that were nearly equal to the GT's but handling that was far superior. As a testament to the car's high-performance aspirations, only a five-speed manual transmission was available (the final drive ratio was 3.45:1).

"Its combination of lighter weight, better chassis and bigger tires gives the SVO a much more tossable character....there's no doubting the SVO is the best-driving Mustang the factory has ever produced," the magazine reported.

Properly driven, the SVO was capable of 15.3-second/90-mph (144.8kph) quarter-mile (402.3m) times, quite respectable for the day. Sixty miles per hour (96.5kph) would come up in less than 7.5 seconds, a bit behind the Mustang GT. Top speed was some 134 mph (215.6kph), according to Ford, though numerous journalists noted that they actually topped out at 127 or 128 mph (204.3 or 205.9kph). Not too shabby for a four-banger.

All wasn't perfect with the SVO, of course. Numerous stories pointed out that the engine was very coarse under hard acceleration. It vibrated mightily, which was completely out of character for a car in this price range. With a base price of $15,585—and enough available options to push the sticker to about $18,000—this was an oversight that should not have been permitted. More refinement was in order.

Sales for the first year did not meet Ford's expectations. It had hoped to restrict sales to fifteen thousand units, but that was a problem it never had to deal with. A total of 4,508 SVOs were produced that first year, a number that had to be disappointing to Ford. And the situation would get worse before it improved.

CHANGE FOR THE BETTER

When the '85 models hit the showrooms, there were few initial changes. The standard rear gearing became 3.73:1 for improved acceleration. A quicker-ratio steering box was fitted, and power locks were part of the base price. Exterior color choices were expanded to include bright red, dark sage, and oxford white. Dark blue metallic was expected but was not offered.

Ford upgraded the SVO for 1985½, blessing it with 30 more horsepower, flush headlights, and Goodyear Eagle tires, among other things. It even dipped in price slightly, making it the quickest and least expensive SVO to date. This did little to help the car, however, as sales plummeted to 1,954.

To get a 140-cubic-inch engine to make 205 horsepower takes quite a bit of doing, and Ford's engineers should be congratulated for what they accomplished,

COMP PREP: HARDCORE SVO

One of the least remembered high-performance Mustangs ever was the SVO with the Competition Preparation option in 1985 and 1986. It was conceived so that the buyer could walk into his local Ford dealership and drive away in an SCCA-ready race machine with license plates. The Comp Prep option deleted many of the SVO's standard features, which not only lowered weight but sliced $1,253 off the sticker price.

Of course, a Comp Prep SVO still cost serious money, but for this outlay of capital you got the most serious Mustang available since the 1965–1966 Shelby GT350 R models. Air conditioning? Forget it; it was history. Power windows? Power locks? Electronic AM/FM stereo search radio? You don't need those things on a race track, and they too were eliminated. You could not order leather seats, either, though one such outfitted car is known to exist.

The disappearance of these popular features created a Mustang that was more than 100 pounds (45.4kg) lighter than the already svelte SVO, and most of that weight came off the front end via the air conditioning compressor and its attendant hardware (this dictated the use of slightly different spring rates).

From the outside, the Comp Prep SVO looked much the same as any other SVO. Sharp-eyed observers, however, would notice that there was a plug on the right front fender where the radio antenna was supposed to go. Inside, there was another block-off plate where the radio used to be, and cranks on the doors for the roll-up windows.

Thanks to a midyear boost in horsepower in '85 and a lower final drive ratio (3.73:1), a Comp Prep SVO could cover the quarter mile (402.3m) in the mid-14-second range at about 95 mph (152.8kph), making it the quickest Fox Mustang produced to that point.

To no one's surprise, this option was not highly publicized. It was offered strictly for homologation purposes and to give hardcore drivers a road course–ready machine. This means that few people bought them when they were available. In two years, just 123 were built—forty in '85 and eighty-three in '86. That makes them exceptionally rare and collectible. For comparison's sake, there were thirty-nine '65 Shelby GT350 R models produced, 107 '93 Cobra Rs, and 252 '95 Cobra Rs.

especially considering the deficiencies that were inherent to the power plant Ford was using. This was a motor designed to move Pintos and other economy-minded vehicles. Stingy fuel consumption, rather than winning races, was its *raison d'être*. It made only 88 horsepower when installed in the 1974 Mustang II, but through perseverance and experimentation, they made it work miracles.

They unleashed the extra ponies that were trapped inside the 2.3 engine through a combination of better engineering and old-fashioned hot-rod know-how. For starters, they used a hotter camshaft, revised intake manifold tract, and larger fuel injectors. The turbocharger itself was carefully reworked to make an extra pound of boost, which may not sound like much, but it was probably good for about 8 to 10 horses in and of itself.

Below: Although the SVO was a capable high performance car, the combination of 210 horsepower and low base price made the GT too seductive for most Mustang enthusiasts to pass up. The GT had a definite negative impact on SVO sales.

It also spooled up quicker, helping eliminate some turbo lag. Instead of a single tailpipe and muffler aft of the catalytic converter, the exhaust split into two pipes. The 205 horsepower came at 5000 rpm, and torque increased significantly as well, from 210 pounds-feet to 248 at 3000 rpm.

Engine vibration and harshness were also greatly reduced by a method that surprised some people. Though many journalists had been clamoring for internal balance shafts, Ford engineers found that they could reduce noise, vibration, and harshness (referred to as NVH in engineering terms) by revising the intake manifold and stiffening the bracketry for air conditioning, power steering, alternator, and so on. According to one publication, the car was now "silky smooth" compared to the earlier version.

A swap from 3.45:1 gears in the differential to 3.73s provided even better torque multiplication and kept the engine revving in or close to its "sweet spot" at all times.

Besides the switch to Goodyear Eagle tires (of the same size as the NCTs), the SVO received revalved shocks and Teflon-lined sway bar bushings, the latter of which took some of the stiffness from the car's ride. Even the Hurst-shift linkage was reworked so that throws were quicker and shorter; clutch pedal throw was also reduced.

A comparison test between the '85½ SVO and the Camaro IROC-Z in *Motor Trend* showed just how greatly improved the car was. Though the Camaro held a slight advantage in acceleration (15.32 in the quarter mile [402.3m] vs. 15.37) and braking, the editors at *Motor Trend* picked the SVO as the winner. "We are mainly seduced by its high-revving, big-hearted little motor and its precise, tight-coupled controls," they said. "Its drivetrain has all the appeal of a Formula Atlantic car: intense, demanding, rewarding (when employed correctly) and fun."

Despite all the SVO's good points, it was becoming very obvious that this model could not compete in the marketplace on a variety of levels. First, few prospective BMW owners were going to switch allegiances to what they perceived to be an inferior product. A BMW was (and to some degree still is) a four-wheeled gold chain, something that you purchase to impress friends and neighbors. No matter how much quicker or better-handling the SVO was, it just didn't have the valet appeal of the "Bimmer" or of other similar imported rides.

Its biggest rival turned out to be the Mustang GT, and dollar for dollar, the V8-powered sister ship was the bargain of the decade. A base price of $10,224 and the rumble of a hot 5.0 helped make the Mustang GT a runaway success. Those in the know opted for the far cheaper (and lighter) LX 5.0 sedan.

For 1986, changes were few. Dark shadow blue became an optional color choice, and sixty-nine SVOs were painted that hue. As did every American car, the SVO got a center high-mounted stop light (the SVO's was mounted in the lower wing of its biplane rear spoiler). Horsepower and torque were rated as being down slightly (to 200 and 240, respectively). Some said this was due to a less aggressive tune in the computer, while others have said there was no detuning whatsoever—that it was just a paper change.

As an interesting side note, the biplane rear spoiler could be deleted for credit. In its place was the GT's decklid-mounted spoiler, painted body color. The reason for this? Ford was running out of the biplane piece, and with the car not coming back for an encore the next year, it saw no reason to whip up another batch.

Popular Hot Rodding magazine did a three-way comparison of turbocharged production cars in its May 1986 issue. This pitted the SVO against a Buick Grand National and a Dodge Conquest sports car. The SVO acquitted itself fairly well, running a 14.67 (corrected) at more than 93 mph, (149.6kph) thus trailing only the Grand National, which clicked off a 14.26 at 95.47 mph (153.6kph). It was tied with the Conquest for quickest through the slalom and had the second-shortest braking distance.

Sales recovered somewhat, to 3,382, but the SVO's time was running out. Sure, there had been plans—big plans—for this heroic automobile. Engineers were working on a dual-overhead-cam (DOHC), four-valve-per-cylinder head for 1987. It was derived from Ford's Mustang GTP race car. Testing in the winter of '86 showed that the engine was capable of producing 280 horsepower, a remarkable 2 per cubic inch. Times for 0 to 60 mph (96.5kph) were in the 5.7 or better range. But in the end, the package was scrapped and the sixteen-valve head was shuffled off to the truck

SVO MUSTANG PRODUCTION

Year	U.S.	Canada	Export	Total
1984	4,263	222	23	4,508
1985	1,498	17	0	1,515
1985½	427	10	2	439
1986	3,314	58	10	3,382
Total	9,502	307	35	9,844

division, where it would be tested on the 2.0L mill and discarded before reaching production.

Ford had exciting changes in store for the 5-liter Mustang, monumental alterations that would not only make it a smash in the showrooms but actually save it as a rear-drive, V8 performance car.

For better or worse, the SVO was deemed a superfluous vehicle. Americans wanted blood-curdling acceleration and whiplash-inducing torque, fuel economy be damned.

There were other factors at work as well. Ford's dealer network never supported the car very much. Many salesmen had no idea what an SVO even was; they were too busy moving LTDs, Tempos, and regular Mustangs to notice. By '86, there was precious little advertising support to drum up interest.

The SVO's three-year production total was 9,844—less than Ford had hoped to sell the first year alone. Still, only a fool would call the SVO a failure. It remains one of the most sought-after Fox Fords.

Opposite: In mid-1985, the SVO got a host of upgrades, not the least of which was a more powerful (205 horsepower) engine. It helped little. Total SVO production for the entire 1985 model year fell by over 50 percent. **Below:** A little-known SVO was the Competition Preparation model. It was introduced in 1985 (this is an '86 version) and was the first American factory road race car since the ZR-1 and ZR-2 Corvettes of 1970 and 1971. Note the lack of a radio in the dash (inset).

4

1987-1993
Cheap Thrills

It ran like a '60s supercar, but did so with a smaller, "smarter" engine. Like a bolt of lightning across the night sky, the 1987 5-liter Mustang electrified enthusiasts. The best part was that no one expected it—not Ford's product planners, not the engineers who designed it, and not the assembly line workers who slapped them together.

But the '87 5-liter Mustang, in both GT and (especially) LX trim, was a bona fide king of the street. It was the quickest damn Mustang in nearly two decades and it came at a price just about anyone could afford.

The Fox-chassis ponycar soldiered on solo in '87; its Mercury cousin, the Capri, had been put out to pasture. Gone too was the much-ballyhooed Mustang SVO, the import fighter the public had deemed too expensive. There were changes galore, the most since its introduction eight years earlier. The interior was completely revamped, its theme echoing the BMW 3-series the SVO tried so desperately to compete against. The exterior was overhauled and its most prominent feature was its SVO-inspired front fascia.

What made the '87 Mustang tick, though, was under the hood. With vastly improved cylinder heads, different pistons, a freer-flowing intake tract, and a slightly larger throttle body, the venerable 5-liter V8 now produced 225 horsepower and 300 rock-and-rollin' pounds-feet of torque. Coupled with the Mustang's light weight, throttle response was instantaneous. Smack the throttle and the tires would howl in protest. It was big-time fun and it didn't take long for the word to get out: the restyled Mustang was one bad hombre; mess with it and you could end up sucking tire smoke.

The second coming of the muscle car could be traced back to a trio of automobiles in 1982: the Camaro Z/28, the Firebird Trans Am, and the Mustang GT. While the first two owed their success to their

2.3L four-cylinder engine (now fuel-injected) that thrashed its way to 88 peak horsepower. It could be ordered with either the five-speed manual or four-speed overdrive transmission. Either way, these were fairly dreadful automobiles, slow and coarse, although they make terrific candidates for V8 swaps today. For the first time in the car's twenty-two-year history, no six-cylinder engine was offered. Continuing a model lineup that had begun a year earlier, all base Mustangs were LXs.

At the top of the line was the Mustang GT, available as both a hatchback and a convertible. It was the wildest-looking ponycar yet, with a bold front air dam that housed a pair of fog lights, lower body skirts, a decklid-mounted wing, and louvered taillamps. As did all Mustangs, the nose featured flush single headlights. On the GT, there was no grille opening; the hood was even with the bumper cover. Out back, a large lower valance was added that echoed the shape of the front air dam. This necessitated the use of different tailpipes on the GT models from those used on the LX. The GT's turned down while the LX's extended straight out past the cover. Convertible GTs did not get a wing; instead they received a decklid-mounted luggage rack.

Standard on the GT were 15- by 7-inch (38.1 by 17.7cm) turbine wheels sporting 225/60VR Goodyear Eagle tires. The GT came standard with upgraded underpinnings, including stiffer variable-rate springs (a touch firmer than on earlier GTs), thick front and rear sway bars, revised gas-pressurized shocks and struts, and quick-ratio, power-assisted steering. The GT/Handling suspension was included on the cheaper LX if you ordered the 5-liter engine, but instead of the turbine-style wheels, the older "phone dial" ten-holers from '86 were used.

Perhaps recognizing the inadequacies of the car's braking system, Ford installed larger 10.84-inch (27.5cm) front discs (with semimetallic pads) for '87, up from 10.06 inches (25.5cm). Much to the dismay of hard drivers, the 9-inch (22.8cm) rear drum brakes were retained and four-wheel disc brakes were not an option (nor would they ever be, though '93 Cobras got them as standard equipment). This handicap would plague the basic 5-liter Mustang until the car was redesigned

Preceding page: The stylists went a little overboard with the '87 GT. The nose echoed the now-deceased SVO but added a huge air dam. The air dam flowed into a rocker extension and a matching rear bumper cover. The lower titanium paint was a no-cost option on all GT models. Louvered taillights debuted on the GT only. **Above:** In contrast to the overdone GT was the clean, uncluttered LX, which with the 5.0 offered more performance for less money. **Opposite:** The popularity of the GT option helped the Mustang soldier on until 1993 (shown), until its Fox-4 replacement was ready. The GT actually outsold the cheaper LX that year.

exceptional handling and drop-dead good looks, the Mustang's popularity was due to its value, acceleration, and spirit. It was just more fun to own and drive. You could toss it around and steer with the throttle, and it didn't cost an arm and a leg. And, as with every Mustang since 1964, you could buy a bare-bones model for the relatively low base price or, option by option, load it up with goodies till your loan officer cried "uncle." It could be *your* Mustang.

Another feature that contributed to the car's increasing popularity was its luggage-swallowing hatchback. Although the Camaro and Firebird were interesting, they were not very practical. Even with a hatchback, they had limited cargo areas. If you ordered a three-door Mustang, though, you could fold down the rear seats and haul just about anything short of a piano. This was an important feature, especially for young Mustang buyers who were starting families. It often meant the difference between purchasing a ponycar and moving on to a more practical (i.e., dull) vehicle.

For 1987, the Mustang offered a variety of different packages to suit most any need. The base car came with a still rather unimpressive version of the

in 1994, when four-wheel discs became standard on the GT. As it was, the Mustang had plenty of go-power but little in reserve when it came to hauling it down from speed.

There was, as mentioned earlier, an entirely new cabin in the Mustang. With the car now in its ninth model year, this was long overdue. Its twin-pod theme had a very European flavor but was still distinctly American. The seats were now the same as those offered in the '84½ 20th Anniversary Limited Edition Mustangs, although they were now equipped with power lumbar supports and adjustable lower side bolsters. A 7000-rpm tachometer with a 6000-rpm redline was fitted, although the speedometer still shut down at 85 mph (136.7kph). Fuel level, battery, coolant temperature, and oil pressure gauges rounded out the instruments, which were now illuminated by green lights instead of red.

A tilt steering wheel was standard and a dead pedal for the driver's left foot was added. The pod directly in front of the driver (behind the steering wheel) contained more modern "flip"-type switches for the headlamps, emergency flashers, fog lights, and rear defroster. Heater, ventilation, and air conditioning (HVAC) controls and the new digital radio were mounted in the center of the instrument panel. The steering wheel was now a two-spoke design that was actually a step backward from what had been in previous Mustangs as far as function goes; it put your hands at the eight-and-four position rather than nine-and-three.

Naturally, the 225-horsepower 5-liter V8 was standard in the GT and the customer had a choice between the T-5 five-speed, which had been beefed up to cope with the increased horsepower and torque, and the automatic overdrive transmission. (Ford had been using Borg-Warner's improved World Class T-5 since 1985, which was stronger than earlier units and had better gear ratios). The 8.8-inch (22.3cm) rear end, introduced in 1986, was available with 2.73:1 gears standard; 3.08 gears were optional for T-5 cars, 3.27s for AOD cars.

Things got even more interesting if you ordered the hot 5-liter engine with the lighter LX trim package. As before, the hot V8 engine was offered in any LX body style—two-door, three-door, or convertible—but without the GT's body cladding and extra features, it was usually about 100 to 140 pounds (45.4 to 63.5kg) trimmer than its more expensive stablemates. Less weight meant even more blistering performance from a car that was already very fast.

How fast? Well, quite a bit faster than one would have expected. The car magazines of the era were trumpeting the Mustang's performance in big, bold headlines. Implausibly, the car was posting acceleration times that were quicker than those of some of the big-bore Mustangs of the 1960s muscle car era. *Hot Rod* magazine, which had declared the 1968½ Cobra Jet 428 Mustang to be the "quickest pure stocker in the land" nearly twenty years earlier, got a five-speed '87 LX to run a 14.17 at 99 mph (159.2kph). In the same test, it clicked off a 6.1-second 0-to-60-mph (96.5kph) run

while pulling .83 g on the skidpad—a road-holding figure unheard of for a production car in 1968.

Cars Illustrated magazine, a small East Coast–based periodical, nearly equaled *Hot Rod*'s time, going 14.18 at 96 mph (154.4kph). As an interesting side note, neither of these test cars was equipped with air conditioning; in fact, the *Cars Illustrated* hatchback, which was privately owned by one of the staff members, was ordered as a radio-delete vehicle (the standard radio was omitted for credit), making it quite rare and very unusual.

The quickest, most incredible time of all was run by *Super Stock & Drag Illustrated* editor Steve Collison, whose black LX coupe ran a 14.02 at 97 mph (156kph) in spite of the fact that it was handicapped by a standard 2.73 rear gear. Had it had the optional 3.08s, it most certainly would have gone in the 13s.

Comparably equipped GT Mustangs typically ran .15 to .20 slower in the quarter mile (402.3m) due to their extra weight. Worse still were the cars using the automatic overdrive transmission. The AOD was never intended to be a high-performance unit, and cars with them ran anywhere from three-tenths to one-half second slower than their T-5 counterparts.

UNDERHOOD HOOFBEATS

Earlier, it was noted that the Mustang received improvements under the hood. Increasing output by 25 horsepower actually takes more effort than one might imagine, given Ford's strict policies governing noise and reliability along with the government's ever more stringent regulations.

The most important change was to the E7TE cylinder heads, which were actually pulled from a 1985 Ford truck engine. They used the same-size valves as the 1986 GT heads but had an unshrouded combustion chamber for a better burn. Larger exhaust ports also contributed to more power. The '86 Mustang's intake tract was also found to be very restrictive as well. Throttle body size was increased from 58mm to 60mm,

---

THE 10-MINUTE TUNE-UP

Entering into 5-liter Mustang vocabulary shortly after the '87s were introduced was the term "10-minute tune-up," which is a series of very simple yet effective modifications that astute 5.0 owners can use to greatly improve performance while spending very little money.

The first order of business is to remove the air silencer located in the inner fender just ahead of the Mustang's air filter. Designed to reduce induction noise, it costs a few horsepower and can just be yanked off. While in there, most 5.0 enthusiasts replace the stock paper air filter with a less restrictive aftermarket part such as the one from K&N Engineering. These two changes alone are usually good for 7 to 10 horsepower.

The next step is to reset the base initial timing from its factory setting of 10 degrees before top dead center (BTDC) to between 13 and 16 degrees. This doesn't necessarily pick up horsepower, but it dramatically improves bottom-end torque. (In fact, many cars were delivered with their timing retarded to about 5 or 6 degrees, which truly hampered performance.)

The last trick is for use only when racing, and that's the installation of a shorter-than-stock accessory drive belt. By using a short belt (70²/₃ inches [179.4cm] in length), you can bypass certain power-robbing accessories and thus free up some horsepower. These tricks combined will usually result in a noticeable seat-of-the-pants improvement while improving your quarter-mile (402.3m) time by three- or four-tenths.

---

and the attendant opening in the upper intake manifold was made appropriately larger.

Contrary to many reports, the camshaft was the same roller piece used since 1985, and though it helped deliver above-average fuel economy and low emissions, it turned out to be a rather decent high-performance part. While the aftermarket continues to offer fine replacement pieces, many modified Mustangs are capable of running in the 10- and 11-second range in the quarter mile (402.3m) with the stock bumpstick.

For an engine that dated back to 1962, the 302 was aging quite nicely. Against all odds, it was remaining emissions-compliant (many engines from various manufacturers fell by the wayside in the late 1970s and the 1980s because their old designs could not be altered to meet tighter emissions standards). But the Windsor V8 soldiered on, slaying dragons while its replacement was being readied.

How did the Mustang stack up against the competition, performancewise? At this point, a stick shift LX could outaccelerate anything on the market short of a Corvette, which cost almost three times as much—and some Mustang "freaks" were running as quick as or quicker than the fastest Vettes. Looking at the hot muscle cars of the day, even a GT could dominate the Chevrolet Monte Carlo SS and the Oldsmobile Cutlass 4-4-2. No iteration of the IROC-Z Camaro or Formula/Trans Am Firebird was close to an LX, though some of these could give the GT a run for its money.

The Mustang LX's closest competitors were the turbocharged and intercooled Buick Grand National and its cousin, the Turbo T-Type. These were ferocious overachievers; despite displacing only 231 cubic inches of V6 engine, they could run in the 14.30–14.50 range bone stock. In late '87, Buick pulled out all the stops and sprung the GNX on an unsuspecting public. Time was running out on General Motors' family of rear-wheel-drive intermediates, and to make sure nobody forgot them, the limited-edition GNX with a bevy of engine and body mods was introduced. They were high-13-second-capable in showroom trim. With a bit of tweaking, the Mustang could run fender to fender with this flyer from Flint, and eventually, Mustang vs. Grand National shootout-type races were happening at drag strips across America.

CHANGES IN THE STABLE

For 1988, the Mustang soldiered on almost unchanged, though some alterations were made. Perhaps it is not shocking that there were so few changes considering that this was the year Ford was supposed to replace the rear-drive Mustang with a front-wheel-drive American-Japanese hybrid designed by Ford and Mazda. This car was slated to be smaller and more fuel-efficient (there were definitely no plans for a V8) and to appeal more to traditional import customers.

When word started to filter out that the next Mustang was going to be a Japanese-based front driver, Ford was deluged with letters, faxes, and phone calls from upset fans of the Mustang who told the company in no uncertain terms how irate they would be if the car underwent such a radical change. Ford reconsidered and the hybrid was introduced as the Ford Probe (Mazda had a less sporty version called the MX-6). The Probe did quite well for itself, and it wasn't long before Ford had two hot sellers in the sporty car segment.

Very early in the '88 model year, the T-top option was discontinued for a variety of reasons. First, the emergence of the convertible five years earlier made it a bit superfluous. Also, these cars were prone to rattles and water leaks. There was also a loss of structural rigidity. The Fox chassis was weakened significantly by the cutouts in the roof, and body flex was a real issue.

Four new colors were added: tropical yellow, almond, bright red, and cabernet red, which was somehow different from 1987's medium cabernet.

The most significant alteration was made on a select group of Mustangs—those headed to California. Because of California's tough emissions regulations (even tougher than the Federal government's), cars destined for the Golden State received special treatment. On these vehicles, engine management was switched from a speed density system to a mass airflow setup. With speed density management, the amount of fuel needed is calculated after the computer receives inputs from the manifold absolute pressure sensor, the air charge temperature sensor, and the throttle position sensor. Mass air systems have a meter that directly measures the amount of air entering the engine and compensates with more or less fuel, depending on the situation. Mass air is slightly more restrictive and cost the Mustang 2 or 3 horsepower (the engine was still rated at 225 hp), but it was more precise, and as enthusiasts discovered, it allowed them far greater latitude when it came to modifying their vehicles.

Mustang convertibles never go out of style. Despite a premium price tag (a GT model like this had a base sticker of $15,852 in 1987 and $21,288 in 1993), they sold like crazy.

MUSTANG COP CARS:
IT TAKES ONE TO CATCH ONE

It wasn't just the general public that craved faster cars in the late 1970s and early 1980s. Police departments were clamoring for them as well. Not that the officers were speed-crazed lunatics—no, the problem was based more on necessity. Police cars had gotten so slow and handled so poorly that they could no longer meet the national standards set for them by the Michigan State Police tests.

The problem was especially dangerous for highway patrol officers, who depended on rapid acceleration in order to merge into the flow of traffic when entering roadways in pursuit of other vehicles. Not only were the police cars of the day not capable of doing this, but when they did get on the road, it often meant a much lengthier (hence more dangerous) pursuit before they caught up with the cars they were after. The full-size and even midsize patrol cars didn't handle well at higher speeds and had even more trouble braking. Some departments took to using two-car teams to apprehend speeders—one

radar car and the other a flag car up ahead. This was dangerous because the officers were sometimes hit or run over as they stood outside the car to flag down the alleged offenders.

The situation became so grave that the California Highway Patrol began testing Chevrolet Camaros for possible purchase as pursuit vehicles. At about the same time, Ford had just introduced the 1982 Mustang GT and prepared a number of two-door Mustang sedans with the 5-liter H.O. engine, upgraded suspensions, and the like for evaluation. The CHP liked them so much that it chose them over the Chevy and ordered 406 of them. Thus was born the Special Service Package Mustang.

What were the differences between the standard Mustang and the SSP version? Surprising to many people was the fact that the engines in the SSPs were identical to those in every other Mustang. Even in 1982, there was adequate power. Instead, the cars were altered to stand up to the more

Imagine the indignity of being pulled over by not just any Mustang highway patrol car, but a Saleen variant. This 1990 example somehow ended up in the Seal Beach, California, cop fleet.

rigorous duty they would see. To handle the myriad battery-draining electrical equipment used in police cars, a heavy-duty alternator was employed. An upgraded cooling system—including silicone hoses, aircraft-style radiator and heater hose clamps, and an air deflector in front of the radiator—kept them from overheating. A certified 160-mph (257.4kph) speedometer fitted to the gauge cluster and a reinforced floor pan were also part of the deal. Both manual and automatic transmissions were offered; the former came with 3.08 gears, the latter with 2.73s.

All of the Mustang's regular production options (RPOs) could be ordered, such as air conditioning and power windows. Limited production options (LPOs), like a 600-watt engine-block heater and a front license plate bracket, were available, as were dealer special-order items like inoperative door courtesy light switches, front door molding delete, radio noise suppression package police radio, paint stripes delete, and a VASCAR speedometer cable.

The Mustang proved itself not only reliable but also quite popular as a police vehicle. About fifteen thousand SSP Mustangs were built from 1982 to 1993, and all except possibly one '82 were notchback models. Many are still in service today, even though it has been more than half a decade since the last one was built.

Among the SSP Mustang's drawbacks were a small interior that could easily be overwhelmed when outfitted with radar guns, shotguns, VASCAR, and police radios, barely leaving room for one officer.

Most cops, however, were overjoyed with the acceleration and handling capabilities (though they were less than thrilled by the marginal brakes). Now they could go out and get the "bad guys," attack off-ramps with aplomb, and, most important, spend precious little time attaining highway speeds and catching up to their prey.

When the new Fox 4–chassis Mustang was introduced in 1994, the exciting Special Service Package was no longer offered. Due to advances in horsepower, handling, and braking, full- and midsize patrol cars (and even some trucks) were again capable of meeting and usually exceeding the standards of the Michigan State Police tests. The smaller, often cramped Mustangs had outlived their usefulness.

Today, the ones that are not in service are highly sought after by both police-car buffs and Mustang enthusiasts.

The Mustang Special Service Package featured:

- Air deflector for front lower radiator
- Remote decklid release relocated to the right of the steering column
- Metal disc-brake rotor shields
- External engine oil cooler
- Reinforced front floor pan (both sides)
- Aircraft-type radiator and heater hose clamps
- Single-key locking system (regular Mustangs used one key for the doors and trunk/hatch and another for the ignition)
- Automatic transmission oil cooler
- Restrictor for the heater hose inlet
- Heavy-duty front seats
- Calibrated 160-mph (257.4kph) speedometer (in 2-mph [3.2kph] increments)
- Full-size spare tire and wheel
- Underhood sound deadener removed

This was a very important change because as the Mustang became more popular with hot-rodders, they learned that the computer management system of the Ford was not only simple to understand or work on, but actually quite adaptable. You could throw all kinds of high-performance parts like superchargers, turbochargers, and camshafts at the engine, and the mass air system would allow the car to continue to run smoothly—something not always possible with a speed-density-type arrangement.

A public grateful for the high-output, rear-drive Mustang responded enthusiastically. A total of 211,225 Stangs rolled out the door that year, an improvement of more than fifty thousand units from '87.

THE END OF AN ERA

That the rear-drive V8 Mustang had gotten a reprieve from Ford's governors was obviously good news to its legion of horsepower-hungry followers. That meant work would have to begin on its successor, because as wonderful and inexpensive as many felt it was, the Mustang had certainly grown long in the tooth. The car was entering its eleventh model year in 1989, a time when many

cars might be on their third complete redesign. In recent memory, only the 1968–1982 Corvette stands out as another example of a car that lasted so long with the same basic underpinnings (and that car's chassis actually dated back to 1963).

While people toiled in secret rooms to map out the Mustang's long-term future, the next few model years had to be mapped out. For 1989, there were only a handful of alterations. Gone was the ridiculous 85-mph (136.7kph) speedometer, replaced with a more useful 140-mph (225.2kph) dial (this was not installed on all '89s; it was a running change during production). The Mustang needed every increment on that gauge, too— and then some. *Car and Driver* published a top speed of 141 mph (226.8kph) in an LX, while *Motor Trend* saw 142 mph (228.4kph) with a GT in its September 1988 test. Obviously, the Mustang was going places, and in a hurry.

There were other interior changes. Mustang LX hatchback models that were ordered with the 5-liter engine received the GT's sport seats as standard equipment. There was also a premium sound system with six speakers and a four-channel amplifier available for just $168. All convertibles were now equipped with power

windows and door locks (the price for the ragtop increased to $14,140 with the four-cylinder engine, $17,001 for the LX 5-liter, and $17,512 for the GT).

One would have expected Ford to pull out all the stops and (with great fanfare) introduce a special twenty-fifth anniversary edition in 1989. One would have been wrong. There had been plans to do so, but the project got shelved and the only hint that this model year was any different from others was a dash plaque affixed to the cars late in the program (March) and continuing through the 1990 model year. If this seems odd, remember that all Mustangs produced from April 17, 1964, until the introduction of the 1966 versions were called 1965s.

Yes, there were plans for a special anniversary edition. According to the *1979–1993 V8 Mustang Reference Guide*, by Al Kirschenbaum, Ford had worked with Roush Industries in Michigan on a feasibility study for a twin-turbo Mustang, but the project bore no fruit. At the same time, work on Ford's high-performance GT-40 cylinder heads was being completed, with an eye on installing them on a limited-production anniversary Mustang. That also fell through, and the heads became available through Ford's SVO Motorsport parts program—though a version would eventually end up on the 1993–1995 Mustang Cobras.

The only underhood change for 1989 was that all 5-liter engines used a mass airflow sensor to measure incoming air for the car's computer management system. It works so well that even today, Mustangs have it on their 4.6L engines.

As the '90s began, Ford kept interest in the Mustang high by further refining the vehicle, increasing its list of standard features, and issuing a series of special editions. Clearcoat paint improved the finish dramatically, and seven new color choices were offered. The mounting point for the front struts was moved rearward toward the windshield to improve tire wear and reduce understeer a bit (thus enhancing handling). Map pouches were added to the doors, rear seat passengers got shoulder harnesses, and the LX 5-liter finally got the GT's left-foot dead pedal.

A driver-side air bag was standard on all Mustangs and was housed in a terrible leather-wrapped wheel that was standard fare in lowly sedans like the Crown Victoria and the Taurus. It was not a proper steering wheel for a car with sporting pretensions, but worst of all, the steering column lost its tilt feature. The wheel was now angled high and toward the driver's face, leaving the Mustang with a poor driving position—one that many people found extremely uncomfortable. Interestingly, the aforementioned cars that shared the Mustang's air bag steering wheel retained the tilt feature. It is believed the Mustang lost it in an effort to offset the cost of the expensive new safety device.

A new options group offered on the GT and V8 LX gave customers air conditioning and power steering, windows, locks, and mirrors, plus cruise control and premium sound with cassette and clock for $1,878. It proved quite popular and was a portent of the future, when many options would be grouped together in less expensive packages. They were (and are) a hit with buyers but to some degree do away with the way Mustang buyers previously "personalized" their cars. There are also far fewer "oddball"-type machines rolling off the assembly lines. Undeniably, the packages saved money for consumers.

The first of the Mustang's limited-edition models was the 1990½ deep emerald jewel green LX convertible. This one got by on looks alone, as there were no mechanical changes to enhance it, although it did come with the GT's turbine-style wheels. Besides the paint color, the LX ragtop got a white leather interior, white console, white dash pad (regular Mustangs came with gray dashes), a white convertible top and top boot, and special body-colored sideview mirrors and body molding.

Ford had hoped to limit sales to thirty-eight hundred, but popularity pushed the number to 4,301.

GOING, GOING...

Despite its advanced age, the accolades kept pouring in for the Mustang. In its 1991 press kit, Ford Public Affairs was proud to point out that *Motor Trend* magazine had called the Mustang GT "one of the top 10 performance cars where cost is an object"; that *Road & Track* named the GT "one of the 10 best cars in the world based on value"; and that *Car and Driver* selected it as one of its "10 Best Cars."

Opposite: What good is a Mustang if it's not painted red? Using this logic, Ford offered three shades of the hue in '91—bright red, medium red, and wild strawberry. **Below:** Ford introduced the first of its series of special convertible Fox Mustangs in 1990 with the Limited Edition LX. Painted deep emerald jewel green, it had matching body moldings and side mirrors, a white leather interior, and the GT's turbine wheels.

High praise, indeed, but as the original Fox Mustang moved closer and closer to the end of its run, Ford kept instituting changes that it hoped would help the car retain its place in such lofty company. For 1991, it offered a twin-spark-plug cylinder head for its 2.3L engine, improving performance from 86 to 105 horsepower. Although this did not make it capable of winning the Indy 500, it allowed the car to accelerate onto freeways without scaring its driver too much.

All GT and 5-liter LX models got pretty new five-star 16- by 7-inch (40.6 by 17.7cm) aluminum rims (for no logical reason, these are sometimes referred to today as "pony" rims). All-season performance tires, P225/55ZR16 all-season Goodyear GT+4 radials, were standard on the LX 5.0. Goodyear's Eagle "gator-backs" forged on as standard on the GT, in the same P225/55ZR16 size used on the LX, but without that tire's compromised performance. To accommodate the new, larger rolling stock, the plastic inner fender liners were reshaped.

It was not widely publicized, but often high-performance Michelin all-season radials were substituted for the Goodyears. Many enthusiasts believe that Goodyears were the only tires installed on Mustangs of this era (1991–1993), but this author did indeed test a GT so equipped in 1992 and found there to be little difference in performance between them and the usual Goodyear.

The convertible was much improved, thanks to a new system that allowed the stack height of the folded top to be 4 inches (10.1cm) lower than before for a cleaner, more attractive appearance.

Ford introduced the second in its series of limited-edition cars in 1992. Again based on the 5-liter LX convertible, this midyear intro was vibrant red with a white top and white interior. It was called the Summer Special; the vibrant red paint was exclusive to this model in '92 and Ford wasn't afraid to use it. The side moldings, mirrors, door trim, and windshield frame were all sprayed this hue.

To further differentiate the Summer Special from other convertibles, a unique decklid wing (with integrated CHMSL) was added. It replaced the luggage rack that was standard on regular ragtop Mustangs.

Like the '90½ green limited-edition Mustang, this one also had a white leather interior. But there were many differences on the new model. The seats had black piping on them and there was a black headliner for the convertible top. Black carpet and dash contrasted with the white interior door panels. The wheels were unique to this model as well; they were painted a pearlescent white.

All these goodies did not come cheap. Ford's suggested retail price was $22,727, the highest of any Fox Mustang to this point and nearly $9,000 more than the GT convertible cost when the droptop model was reintroduced in 1983. That didn't stop 2,019 people from snapping them up when the Summer Specials hit the showrooms (production was limited by the manufacturer, not supply and demand).

Not much else was new in 1992. There was a new dome light standard with dual map lights; optional features included a four-way adjustable driver's seat and a revised premium sound system. Otherwise, Ford was playing a waiting game until the 1994 Mustang was ready.

Cynics would later point out that this alteration would—on paper, at least—make the 215-horsepower rating of the new 1994 Mustang GT look a little better. And when Ford could squeeze only 215 horses from the all-new 4.6L single-overhead-cam (SOHC) V8 in the '96 GT, it looked less like the flop that it was; after all, it had equaled the mighty 5.0.

Later in the 1993 model year, however, Ford would unleash four prized Mustangs: a pair of limited-edition convertibles, a hot new Cobra, and an even more scorching race-only pony, the Cobra R.

First, the convertibles. There was no special name for these machines and they were brought to the market with little, if any, fanfare. But with bright colors unique to these models, they were hard to ignore.

One was canary yellow clearcoat with a chromed version of the GT/5.0 LX five-spoke rims. Either a black or white leather interior was available, and the top matched the color of the seats. Its sister car could have been called the ice cream wagon. The body, top, seats, and wheels were all white. Unlike regular Mustangs that year, which were painted vibrant white, this car had its own color, oxford white.

The seats in both editions were unusual in that they had galloping horses embroidered into the headrests. There were also special floor mats. Like the '92½ vibrant red special edition, the side moldings, windshield frame, and side mirrors were all body color. They also received a small decklid wing rather than a luggage rack.

Pricing on both cars was a tad high. The white version was $21,709, and the yellow car (probably because of its polished wheels) was a bit more expensive at $22,221. They were definitely limited-production automobiles, with fifteen hundred oxford white cars and 1,503 canary yellow cars manufactured.

As nice as these rare ragtops were, they paled in significance to the '93 Cobra and Cobra R. Although these cars will be covered in great detail in chapter six, they were milestone vehicles and will get some mention here.

The Cobra and the F-150 Lightning truck were the first vehicles launched by Ford's Special Vehicle Team,

Opposite: Thanks to runaway support from the automotive aftermarket, Mustang owners could customize their cars in an infinite number of ways, from trick wheels to complete engines and superchargers. **Above:** Saleen celebrated its tenth anniversary in 1993 with a limited-edition SA-10 Mustang. It had unique paint and could be ordered with any high-performance part in the Saleen catalog. Base price was $36,995.

THE END

To Ford's credit, it didn't let the Fox Mustang's passing occur without a flourish of exciting, perhaps collectible, cars being introduced. No, the base Mustang had little in the way of anything new for '93; according to the '93 Ford press kit, the only difference was a new four-speaker stereo. The 5-liter engine itself now employed aluminum hypereutectic pistons instead of forged aluminum slugs, although this had no effect on power output. The most unusual move was that the horsepower rating on the 5-liter engine was now reduced to 205 (torque was down from 300 pounds-feet to 275). Various explanations have been offered as to why, but the two official reasons are that Ford slightly altered its testing procedure and that the 205 rating more accurately reflected power lost since 1987 to slight mechanical changes.

the spiritual successor to the failed Special Vehicle Operations group that delivered the SVO Mustang in 1984. SVT was formed to produce upscale, limited-production, high-performance machines to be sold through a specially trained network of SVT dealers around the country. It cost extra to become an SVT dealer, and less than 25 percent of Ford dealers nationwide opted into the program (even fewer survive today).

What made the Cobra so special? There were numerous items. The car received special bodywork, including a unique grille and rear spoiler, plus 17-inch (43.1cm) wheels and tires (a first on a Fox Mustang), four-wheel disc brakes, a more compliant suspension, and a specially prepared 5-liter V8 that used Ford's excellent GT-40 cylinder heads and a cast version of the GT-40 intake (among other hi-po goodies).

Though they were rated at 235 horsepower, they performed more like they had 270. Magazines of the day were clicking off 13-second elapsed times, with the best coming from *Muscle Mustangs & Fast Fords* (13.75 at 98.27 mph [158.1kph]).

Only three colors were offered—vibrant red, teal metallic, and ebony—and all had gray interiors, the majority of them in leather.

As for the R model, this was the first Mustang to wear a "race-only" designation since the 1965 Shelby GT350R. The car was built with a number of features to homologate it for SCCA and IMSA racing, including larger disc brakes, heavy-duty shocks and struts, and 17- by 8-inch (43.1 by 20.3cm) wheels. A number of standard features and creature comforts were left off the '93 R, including air conditioning, radio, back seat, and rear defogger, all in the name of light weight. (The lack of these items also helped prevent the cars from falling into the wrong hands, i.e., nonracers or those who might attempt to drive them on the street. Thanks to

Above: SVT Cobra owners are a finicky bunch and like to keep their cars perfect—if they can (note the bra to protect the nose from stone chips).
Inset: Ford gave Mustang enthusiasts an unknowing peek into the future with the 1993 Cobra R wheel. In unpainted form, it was actually the optional 17-inch wheel for the 1994–1995 Mustang GT.

their special springs, shocks, and struts, these cars would be unlivable on the street to all but the most hard-core enthusiast.)

Both the production Cobra and the Cobra R were smashing success stories. Nearly five thousand street Cobras were built and sold (4,993), and 107 R models were produced (many of which saw track duty, albeit unsuccessful).

Most important, they proved that there was indeed a market for a hard-charging, high-priced specialty Mustang. Unlike the SVO, the Cobra would go on to meet or exceed its sales targets.

The last '93 Fox Mustang left the Dearborn assembly plant on August 26 of that year. In its place, Ford was offering a greatly improved car, the SN95, also known as the Fox-4 Mustang. But something definitely died that day in Michigan. The '94 Mustang was a far better vehicle, but it was quite a bit more expensive, and it was slower. Sure, it was still darn fast and cost half as much as a new Corvette. But the Mustang as the standard bearer of cheap speed was gone. Still, there were more than two and a half million 1979–1993 Fox cars built, and they are highly sought after by countless ponycar enthusiasts.

Below: In 1993, the Cobra was reintroduced in three colors: black, red, and teal, the latter being a one-year-only offering. **Following pages:** The last of the "limited edition LX" Fox Mustang convertibles were either oxford white with white wheels and white interiors, or canary yellow with your choice of black or white leather interiors, a top that matched the interior, and chrome "pony" rims.

5

1994–1998
Twenty-First–Century Fox

 One of the most challenging assignments in the automotive industry is to redesign a wildly successful car. In the 1990s, it costs upward of $1 billion to bring a completely new car to market. If the team responsible for this project fails, the stakes obviously are very high.

When it comes time to overhaul a legend like the Mustang, the job is even more nerve-racking. The Mustang isn't a car; it is an icon—to some a way of life, even a religion. Millions of enthusiasts are counting on it. There are decades of history to live up to. There are ghosts everywhere.

In some ways, it is easier to design a car from scratch than it is to reinvent a cult hero. With a family sedan, you just have to make it roomier, more practical, more fuel-efficient, and inoffensive. Accomplish these goals, and with some help from the marketing department, you'll have a success on your hands.

Now imagine the task of Team Mustang. The members of this group drew a dream assignment, but the eyes of the world were upon them. No one cares if you screw up a Ford Aspire. But the Mustang is Ford's image leader around the globe. Strike out and it's back to designing turn-signal stalks for Escorts in the sub-sub-sub-sub-basement.

Mustang enthusiasts are a loyal and faithful bunch. Many have been purchasing the cars since Lyndon Johnson was president. Heck, even Bill Clinton owns a '67 coupe. Hundreds of clubs all over the world celebrate the original ponycar, and unlike a Corvette or a Porsche, which are single-purpose, high-performance vehicles, the Mustang is many different things to many different people.

To some, it is a fire-breathing hot rod; to others, a youthful runabout to take to the country club or something in which to escape for the weekend. It can be an economical second car or an all-out race machine.

Team Mustang's goal was to deliver a modern, efficient version of the car America had adopted as its own, one with all the virtues and precious few of the flaws. At the same time, economics dictated that it had to use the same basic Fox platform that was originally introduced to the public in the fall of 1977 underneath the Ford Fairmont and Mercury Zephyr. The big question was simple: how much life was left in the old Fox platform?

As it turns out, enough to extend the Mustang's life into the twenty-first century.

One of the Mustang's biggest faults was that the Fox chassis wasn't as rigid as it needed to be. A flexible chassis is the source of many ills, including squeaks, rattles, and vibrations. In the case of convertibles, add cowl shake and water leaks to the mix. When it comes to ride and handling, engineers must overcompensate for these weaknesses. The end result is usually a ride that is way too harsh and a chassis that can't be optimally tuned for a variety of real-world conditions.

With the 1994 Mustang, Ford's engineers took much of what they had learned about fortifying the Fox chassis from earlier, more expensive Thunderbird and Cougar variants and applied the knowledge to the new Mustang. That meant a host of improvements and a structure that was 56 percent stiffer in bending and 44 percent stiffer in torsion than the earlier Fox cars. The increased rigidity gave engineers more leeway to tune the chassis and make it behave properly under a variety of conditions.

The new platform was called Fox-4—Fox for the fact that it was still based on that chassis, 4 for the model year in which it was introduced, 1994. Still, according to Ford, of the 1,850 parts that made up the Mustang, 1,330 were new.

"This is not a carryover platform," said Will Boddie, Ford's Director, Small and Midsize Car Segment, at the time of the '94 Mustang's introduction. The car couldn't be totally new, he said, because "affordability is a big part of what a Ford Mustang is. When we talked with Mustang owners during the development of the car, they kept saying, 'What can you do to keep it affordable, to give us value.' We listened to them."

Unfortunately, it also meant the elimination of the hatchback from the model lineup. Ford's explanation was that it was "very difficult, if not impossible" to build a torsionally stiff three-door hatchback. What Ford meant was that it was very difficult, if not impossible, to build one on the aging Fox platform; in fact, other manufacturers, including the Japanese, were successfuly building three-door hatchback sports cars on entirely new chassis designs.

Still, the new Fox-4 Mustang coupe soldiered on with more of a fastback design, and the convertible returned as well, now as a vastly improved vehicle.

To accomplish its twin goals of increased structural integrity and improved ride and handling, engineers

Preceding pages: The 1994 Mustang borrowed heavily from its first-generation (1965–1973) ancestors. Note the open-mouthed grille and C-shaped side indentation. **Opposite:** The three styling themes for the SN95 Mustang were the Rambo (top), Schwarzenegger (center) and Jenner (bottom). The Schwarzenegger was chosen.

JENNER, RAMBO, AND SCHWARZENEGGER: STYLING THE '94 MUSTANG

Unlike with the previous-generation Mustang, Ford made a conscious effort to draw inspiration from the past when it came to styling the new ponycar. The 1979–1993 cars bore little, if any, family resemblance to the Mustangs of 1965–1978. This certainly did not hurt it from a sales standpoint, but Ford played it close to the vest with the '94 Mustang.

Eventually, it boiled down to three themes. Around 1990, a clean (if uninspiring) design was shown to clinics. According to Ford, it was dubbed the Bruce Jenner because it was trim and athletic. It received a lukewarm reception, attractive to some for many of the same reasons people liked the Probe. To Ford, this meant the car was too "Japanese" and appealed to the wrong buyer.

A second theme was wild and aggressive, with scoops, wings, and spoilers. Said Bud Magaldi, Mustang Design Manager, "It was a Batmobile-type of thing, a very aggressive car that was gutsy and dramatic, like a Stealth Bomber." From an enthusiast's point of view, this car, dubbed Rambo, was a winner. It was mean and bold, but Ford judged it too far out for the mainstream market.

The winning concept was somewhere between the Bruce Jenner and the Rambo, and looked like "a Bruce Jenner that went down to the gym and put on some muscle and bulk," according to Magaldi. Hence this concept was dubbed the Arnold Schwarzenegger.

Those interviewed said they preferred this last theme because the car had scoops, and even with the horses off, it looked like a Mustang. Ford claims that it kept enthusiasts' comments in mind when the forty-person design team went to work on fine-tuning the Schwarzenegger concept for production.

"Our goal was to bring back the Mustang heritage in a very contemporary way. That was the key," Magaldi said.

Left: The Jenner model was deemed too soft, too generic, and too Japanese. If you look at the rear quarter window, there is also a hint of the ill-fated Mustang II. **Below:** This late model is very close to what the production '94 Mustang became. Rear wing and wheels are obvious differences. **Opposite:** Though the Rambo was pronounced too aggressive, many of its styling cues made production on the '99 Mustang, the SN95's first major redesign, including the headlight/marker light and fender flares.

10-18-90
S-32099—9

implemented a number of changes on the new model. Much heavier-gauge metals were used in the rocker panel areas for both the coupe and convertible. Two heavy-gauge longitudinal reinforcements and several strategically placed internal bulkheads were added to each of the convertible's rocker panels. About a dozen add-on gussets or reinforcements were used where necessary in both body styles. A deep-drawn

inverted-U channel and members ran transversely from B-pillar to B-pillar on top of the floor panel.

According to Ford, significant gains were made in the stiffness of the '94 by incorporating box-section roof headers and rails (longitudinal members). Previously, they had been formed with open sections.

Convertibles got a reinforced windshield frame, and to further eliminate cowl shake, body structure engineers bolted an X-brace to the bottom of the car. All Mustangs now used what the aftermarket called a strut tower brace to tie the strut towers to the car's cowl.

Above: One area on the new car that was criticized was the rear styling treatment, especially the three-bar horizonal taillights. **Inset:** The interior of the '94 Mustang was a triumph, echoing the themes of the Ford Mach III concept car, 1960s Mustangs, and mostly, the '63–67 Corvette Sting Rays. **Opposite:** This laser red GT has the optional 17-inch (43.2cm) wheels and Goodyear tires. **Opposite, inset:** The 5.0 engine used the Thunderbird's low-profile intake, which cost it a few horsepower.

RIDING HORSEBACK

For improved handling, the car was given a slightly longer wheelbase, a wider track, and new front suspension geometry. Four-wheel disc brakes were thrown in as standard equipment, and an antilock feature was optional.

The front crossmember was moved forward and the control arms were slightly longer on the 1994 Mustang. The results were a wheelbase that was ¾ inch (1.9cm) longer and improved steering and suspension geometries. Track width was increased by a whopping 3.7 inches (9.4cm) on the base model and 1.9 inches (4.8cm) on the GT. These suspension geometry changes, said Ford, would result in better handling and reduced tire wear. Front caster was increased from 1.5 to 4.0 degrees, improving directional stability, while the wider front track sharpened steering response and increased cornering grip. Sway bars were now tubular to reduce weight.

Out back, the rear suspension was basically a carryover from before, though a sway bar was used on the non-V8 car for the first time.

Power-assisted rack-and-pinion steering was standard on all Mustangs, and thankfully, the tilt feature was not only back but standard on all models.

With the introduction of the new Mustang, Ford simplified its lineup. Gone was the LX designation. The choices were a base Mustang with a V6 engine in coupe or convertible, or a V8-powered GT in the same body choices. Fifteen-inch (38.1cm) wheels and tires were standard on the V6 car, whereas the hairier GT got 16-inch (40.6cm) aluminum wheels with Firestone Firehawk tires as standard equipment, with 17-inch (43.1cm) alloy wheels and Goodyear Eagles optional.

The interior was also completely revamped for the 1994 model. Its twin-pod theme echoed the Mustangs of the '60s, the Mach III show car of 1993, and especially the 1963–1967 Corvette Sting Ray. For a cohesive effect, the door panels and instrument panel (IP) were designed together as a single, flowing unit. Sculpted armrests and map pockets on the doors carried the shape and theme of the IP.

The driver-side pod contained full gauges, including a 140-mph (225.2kph) speedometer on the GT. The steering wheel was a thick, four-spoke design that housed an air bag. But unlike the previous car's air bag wheel, this new design was decidedly more sporting in nature, with properly placed spokes at the nine- and three-o'clock positions. It was as good as the 1990–1993 one was bad.

In the center of the IP were the HVAC controls and the radio (AM/FM/cassette was standard). Both were placed high enough to be user-friendly, another quantum leap ahead of earlier Fox Mustangs. A digital clock was housed in its own pod on the top, in the center of the dash. The passenger-side pod housed an air bag and a fairly spacious glove box. Other nice touches were an auxiliary buss for cellular phones, radar detectors, and the like; a roomy center console with a pull-out cup holder; and "soft-touch" plastics for buttons, knobs, and certain surfaces.

The rear seats folded down, allowing access to the trunk, but because the hatchback was gone, storage space was reduced and far more difficult to access. The decklid opening was fairly narrow, and with the seats up, the trunk was rather small. With the seats down, the situation improved, but not up to the station wagon–like proportions of previous Fox Mustangs.

When it came down to how the car would look, Ford took a conservative approach. It would borrow heavily from Mustangs of the 1960s while at the same time avoiding the trap of creating an old-fashioned-looking car. The stylists were also wary of designing a small car that was "too Japanese-looking." About the only thing they knew going in was that the car would share the long-hood/short-deck theme that had appeared on Mustangs almost thirty years earlier.

"When we talked with Mustang owners they kept telling us that we should capture the heritage of the original Mustangs," said Magaldi. "And if there was one element that was brought up again and again, it was that the design should be American."

Magaldi's group had an interesting challenge: make it contemporary, make it sophisticated, but don't make it too soft. The car had to have muscles, both under the hood and to the naked eye. In an interesting move, Ford had Mustang club members, Mustang magazine editors, and the members of the general public take part in consumer clinics beginning in 1989, and the company quickly learned what the faithful wanted.

When the '94 Mustang was unveiled, it received plenty of praise. The car had the open-mouth grille with a galloping horse in the center and the C-shaped side indentations instantly recognizable to fans of the 1965–1968 Mustang. But the car had a purposeful look, one that was at the same time tough and elegant. Unlike the new Camaro and Firebird, which had been introduced a year earlier and were boy-racer all the way, the Mustang was a nice compromise. While some enthusiasts felt it was too "soft," most felt that the car found the often-elusive tasteful area between totally hot and middle-of-the-road bland.

On the downside, the car was larger than its predecessor, and thus a few hundred pounds heavier. This was the result of not only the extra size, but also the extra chassis bracing and stiffeners that were added.

One styling cue that was pretty much universally panned was the rear end treatment. While the bulk of the car was an interesting mix of curves and shapes, the back of the car looked like a guillotine had come down on it. It was square, with nary a shape to it, and rather tall. Also, the car's ride height was unusually high. The wheel wells were huge, and even with the optional 17-inch (43.1cm) tires, there were large gaps between the tops of the tires and the wheel well openings.

POWER TO THE PEOPLE

The most controversial part of the new Mustang was its choice of power plants. While the base car's standard 3.8-liter V6 engine was widely praised as a quantum leap over the awful 2.3L four, the world was left perplexed by the GT's 215-horsepower 5-liter V8. Horsepower was—on paper, at least—up by 10, but the car's newfound bulk made it far slower than earlier

WORLD CLASS TIMING

When the press first saw the new Mustang, Ford boasted of how quickly the car was brought into production—World Class Timing, Ford called it.

According to Ford, the first '94 Mustang would roll off the assembly line on October 4, 1993, just thirty-five months after the project received the official go-ahead from management.

World Class Timing was introduced to significantly cut down development time, ergo costs, but at the same time Ford felt that by reacting more quickly, it could bring to market the vehicles customers wanted when they wanted them.

The two biggest changes to how Ford would be doing business were that all Team Mustang members worked under one roof, and they all were dedicated to just this project and no others.

"A fundamental element of World Class Timing is to have the people who make the decisions housed together with the people who execute those decisions on a daily basis," according to Mike Zevalkink, the Mustang Program Manager at the time.

The idea was to eliminate as much paperwork and as many meetings as possible. Over time, this allowed Team Mustang to cut the number of engineering prototypes from three to two, to cut five months from the normal tooling time for major body panels, and to speed up design and color-and-trim work.

Certainly, the Mustang's quick development was aided by the fact that it used existing engines and a modified existing chassis. Ford spent "only" $700 million to bring the new Mustang to market, about half of which went toward retooling the assembly plant.

The SN95 ushered in a new era in how Ford designs and builds cars.

5-liter Mustangs. It was backed by either the T-5 five-speed manual gearbox or the AOD-E, an electronically controlled four-speed automatic.

While the SN95 was being developed, Ford had introduced a new family of engines, the 4.6L overhead-cam modular V8s. There were two different power plants. One was an SOHC engine that originally saw duty in the large Ford Crown Victoria and Mercury Marquis but would soon show up in the Thunderbird and Cougar and in other large cars. There was also a much more powerful DOHC version introduced in the new Lincoln Mark VIII, capable of a robust 280 horsepower.

Many enthusiasts expected more powerful versions of both engines to appear in the SN95 Mustang. During the Mustang's gestation period, the Camaro and

Opposite: Journalists first got to drive the 1994 Mustangs at a special preview in Solvang, California, at an actual working ranch. Over a varied and beautiful route, the new car proved itself a much improved, although slower, car.

Firebird had been brought to the market with 275-horsepower examples of the Corvette's LT1 V8. This robust engine was available with the stout Borg-Warner T56 six-speed manual or a bang-screech electronic four-speed overdrive automatic, putting the General Motors twins in an enviable position.

At the very least, the Ford faithful hoped the '93 Cobra's GT-40-ized engine would be standard in the GT, with a hot 5.8L V8 optional in the Cobra. Instead, they got what amounted to the 5-liter V8 that had formerly seen duty in the Thunderbird. It even shared that car's low-profile intake manifold, thanks to a lower hoodline, though Ford claimed that it actually improved flow somewhat.

Bolstering the Bird's 5-liter engine was the '93-earlier H.O. camshaft, a larger mass air meter, less restrictive headers, and a much improved exhaust system. A lighter, more efficient electric drive cooling system also freed up a few ponies.

From a performance standpoint, the new GT couldn't hold a candle to the Z/28/Trans Am/Formula ponycars. The Chevy/Pontiac twins destroyed the Mustang GT in acceleration; they also outhandled and outstopped it.

The Mustang's virtues were its more accommodating interior, its styling, and, ultimately, its legacy. In the sales race, the Mustang trounced its rivals, outselling its two competitors combined.

HOOVES OF THUNDER

The SN95 Mustang was an instant sales success, even though it arrived in showrooms in the dead of winter, which is typically a terrible time of year for sporty car sales in general and rear-drive muscle car sales in particular. Ford had little problem selling the Fox-4 cars, even against excellent competition from General Motors.

Questions for enthusiasts remained: how fast was the new car? Could it compete in a straight line with the mighty new F-body twins from Chevy and Pontiac?

Unfortunately, it was in this regard that the GT fell short. It was still plenty quick and powerful, but the

INTRODUCING FOX-4: MUSTANG MEETS THE MASSES

On December 27, 1993, the new Mustang officially went on sale to an anxious public. But Ford didn't just deliver cars to the showrooms or buy some ad time on television.

No, Ford cashed in on all the loyalty and goodwill that had been built up with Mustang enthusiasts. Two months earlier, Ford threw the Mustang a gala coming-out party—one hundred of them, actually. In an unprecedented move, Ford hosted car shows with local Mustang clubs in one hundred cities across the United States. The date was October 17, 1993—twenty-nine years and six months after the original ponycar shocked the country, and nearly fifteen years to the day since the Fox Mustang's debut.

Millions of people from coast to coast saw the new car on television. Newspaper articles heralded its arrival the next day, and the timing of the event was such that magazine articles appeared to coincide with the car's on-sale date.

Not surprisingly, thousands of people in key markets turned out to find out what the Mustang of the future would be like.

One of the places was Flushing, New York, at the site of the 1964 World's Fair—the very place the first production Mustang was unveiled. Right there, under the same Unisphere, the cover was pulled back on seven Fox-4 Mustangs. A wildly enthusiastic crowd rushed to get a glimpse of the vehicles, which were accompanied at the party by eight dozen classic Mustangs and Fords of the '60s. According to a Ford spokesman on hand that day, some 500,000 of the six million Mustangs ever built—one in every twelve—were sold in the New York metropolitan area.

Other cities included Los Angeles, where 305 classic Mustangs and the Goodyear Blimp turned out, Chicago (Soldier Field), and Minneapolis (the Mall of America).

Above and right: The tonic for the horsepower-deprived again proved to be the Cobra, a spring '94 intro. Output was now rated at 240 for the Cobra-ized 5.0, an all-time high (though 270 was actually closer to the true output). **Opposite:** Ford responded to complaints by Mustang traditionalists and replaced the horizontal taillights of 1994–1995 with vertical units for '96, as seen on this non-production car.

'94's added weight put additional strain on the 5-liter engine. Further, the car was so smooth and refined that it didn't feel as fast. This was a mixed blessing. There was no comparing the new Fox-4 Mustang to its old Fox-based predecessor. It was a quantum leap forward.

One of the drawbacks, however, was a significantly higher price and a less sprightly feel. The 1987–1993 cars bristled with unbridled performance. They were unbalanced but fun and, at about $15,000 and change for a 5-liter LX coupe, a bargain. The '94 Mustang GT stickered at a shade under $18,000 and with a few options could easily cost more than $21,000—order a convertible GT with leather and an automatic transmission and you were looking at more than $25,000.

So how quick was the '94 Mustang? Barry Shepard, a Ford truck engineer, ran a five-speed version in the Pure Stock class of the International Hot Rod Association (IHRA). With nothing more than a set of 26-by 8.5-inch (66 by 21.5cm) slicks and bumped timing, his car ran a 14.23 at 95.68 mph (153.9kph).

A few months later, *Muscle Mustangs & Fast Fords* magazine tested a nearly identically equipped car, but a '95 instead of a '94. With stock timing and street tires, the car scorched its way to a 14.45 at 94 mph (151.2kph). This proved once and for all that the engine was definitely not down on power compared to the earlier Fox cars. Its weight, however, was some 200 pounds (90.8kg) heavier than an old LX, which would in part account for the elapsed time being a few tenths slower.

Still, for a fully optioned automobile, this was inspiring performance. The car was not in Z/28 territory yet, but it appeared to be headed in that direction. Ford's Camaro-thrasher would arrive slightly later in the '94 model year and would come dressed in Cobra-skin duds.

As with the '93 Cobra, Ford's Special Vehicle Team outfitted the 5-liter engine with an onslaught of GT-40 power goodies, a slightly different appearance, and a reworked suspension. The end result of these changes was a 240-horsepower car that would run high-13-second quarter-mile (402.3m) times off the showroom floor, even on street tires.

And for the first time since 1970, the Cobra Mustang was offered as a convertible. All were dressed in Indianapolis Pace Car livery and all were painted Rio red. All was right in the Mustang universe.

WHAT'S NEW?

For the Mustang, the 1995 model year was nothing more than a carryover. The late intro of the '94 dictated that few changes were needed. The real bummer was that 1995 would be the last year for the beloved 5-liter engine in the Mustang. For '96, Ford was making a complete changeover to modular 4.6L power in V8 applications.

Ford did manage to prove that there was still life left in the antediluvian pushrod engine family. Two new players came to the game, a pair whose goal was, seemingly, to ensure that the general public didn't forget the legacy of the Windsor V8s. The first was the Mustang GTS, which was the spiritual successor to the old LX 5-liter. From the outside, it was almost—but not quite—a twin to the GT, even sharing that car's fender badges. Gone were the rear spoiler and fog lights. Only the standard 16-inch (40.6cm) wheels and tires were offered.

Inside, the base six-cylinder car's interior was all that was available. That meant cheaper cloth seats (sans power features) and no leather steering wheel, and although power windows and locks were optional, the objective was to offer a cheaper ponycar, so the power features weren't encouraged.

The GTS was a few pounds lighter than the GT and, if you stayed away from the options, definitely cheaper. The base price was just $16,910, or $3,010 less than a GT with the preferred equipment package. Strangely, Ford did almost nothing to promote this vehicle. There were no press releases, print ads, or television commercials. As far as we can tell, Ford's southern

California press pool (where media types get cars to test and photograph) was the only bureau of its type to stock one. This author drove that car for a week, and while there was no opportunity to drag test it, the GTS felt much more flingable than the GT. Like the old LX, it was a ripper, with the penalty being a rather bargain-basement cabin and smaller tires.

The second gunslinger was an all-out freak of the automotive business, the Cobra R. Like the '93 version, this car was set up for racing—no radio, no air conditioner, no back seat. But there was more. Instead of the 5-liter Cobra engine, the R model got a GT-40-ized 351-cubic-inch monster motor producing 300 horsepower and 365 pounds-feet of torque. It also received a much better suspension, beautiful five-spoke wheels, and a 20-gallon (75.7L) fuel cell. Ford was determined to build a car that would crush the Firebird Formulas in SCCA and IMSA road racing competition, and if that meant building an ultrarare, ultraexpensive ringer, then so be it.

The '95 will be covered in depth in chapter six, but suffice it to say that it was the fastest, most brutish Fox Mustang to that point, and as of this writing, Ford still hasn't come out with a quicker modular Mustang. With a $35,000 price tag and production limited to 252 cars (250 of which were sold to the general public), the R model was the object of much controversy. Many felt since it was a street-legal car that met all federal regulations, the 5.8L engine should have been offered in all Mustangs.

Also, there was some hand-wringing over whether Ford was resorting to cheating. After all, it had to build a special-edition car at a price that made it the most expensive Mustang ever to be competitive with a run-of-the-mill $18,000 Firebird. Still, no one complained when *Muscle Mustangs & Fast Fords* tested one with slicks in its October 1995 issue and ran a 12.91 at 103.61 mph (166.7kph), or when a Steeda Autosports–prepared version started winning races.

Sales of the SN95 Mustang were robust. Some 123,198 were moved in the abbreviated 1994 model year, and in 1995 a very grand total of 185,985 found homes. Fox-4 was a rousing success. The big question was whether the momentum could be sustained: would the 4.6L GT and Cobra help sales or hurt?

Above: The 4.6-liter single-overhead-cam V8 replaced the venerable 5.0 in '96 but couldn't match the old engine's performance. **Opposite:** The SN95 Mustang got its first styling update in 1996. The grille had a honeycomb insert, the 17-inch wheels echoed those on the Mach III show car, and the vertical taillights returned.

GOODBYE PUSHRODS, HELLO OVERHEAD CAMSHAFTS

At the introduction for the 1996 Mustangs, anticipation was understandably high. For only the second time in the car's thirty-plus-year history, a Windsor Ford small-block would not be available in any model. (The first time was with the 1974 Mustang II, which was not available with a V8 engine. The 302 did, however, return to the options sheet for 1975.)

This time around, the relatively new 4.6L modular (or Romeo) power plant was the V8 of choice, and came in two very distinct flavors. The first was the SOHC, two-valve-per-cylinder engine, which produced 215 horsepower at 4200 rpm and 285 pounds-feet of torque at 3500. It was standard equipment in the GT and was backed by either of two new transmissions, the five-speed T-45 from Borg-Warner or the 4R70W, a four-speed automatic pirated from the Lincoln Mark VIII.

Those with extra coin and a serious speed jones opted for the DOHC Cobra. This car's all-aluminum engine featured four-valve-per-cylinder technology, a block cast in Italy, and assembly by special hand-picked teams at Ford's Romeo, Michigan, engine plant.

Ford boasted of the high technology inherent to both of these mills, but enthusiasts were more interested in how they performed. In short, the SOHC GT was a major disappointment, and the thirty-two-valve Cobra was damn impressive. The GT, while having the same output as the 5-liter cars on paper, did not perform nearly as well, with 0-to-60-mph (96.5kph) and quarter-mile (402.3m) times both off by about half a second—a veritable eternity in performance terms. As *Car and Driver* succinctly put it, "The Mustang GT has a new heart, but it's not Tarzan's."

Part of its problem was that while it made the same amount of torque as the 5-liter, its peak came at a much higher rpm. And although the car had an SOHC design—which usually means great high-rpm performance—the engine fell flat on its face shortly after 4200 rpm.

The 4.6 2V was also the victim of puny valves (1.75 inches [4.4cm] on the intake side and 1.34 inches [3.4cm] on the exhaust) and restrictive cylinder heads and exhaust manifolds. Whereas the old 5-liter cars came equipped with genuine tube headers for improved exhaust scavenging, the 4.6 GT had old-fashioned, lo-po cast manifolds (a nod toward tightened emissions controls and packaging concerns).

Fortunately, the Cobra's engine was far superior. With twice as many valves, a vastly improved combustion chamber design, and a better intake manifold (among numerous other improvements), it could rev to 6800 rpm. The hand-built engine produced 305 horsepower at 5800 rpm and put out 300 pounds-feet of torque at 4800.

The new Cobra was a mean hombre, and the quickest of the lot were capable of mid- to low-13-second quarter-mile (402.3m) times in street trim when driven properly. Strangely, there is a wide disparity in the performance of these cars. While this author has witnessed some run 13.30s, others have been stuck in

the 13.90–14.00 range, with trap speed varying from 101 to more than 103 mph (162.5 to 165.7kph).

Thanks to the dimensions of the 4.6 engine, the front suspension of the modular Mustangs needed to be redesigned. The 4.6 is taller than the 5.0 and requires more space on the bottom as well, so Ford designed a new front crossmember that not only provided additional strength and rigidity to the structure, but at the same time revised the front end geometry that reshapes the dynamic curves for caster and camber. The end result was superior steering feel, improved steering response, and improved tire wear.

Visually, the Mustang received noticeable changes. The optional 17-inch (43.1cm) wheels for the GT were now a sharp five-spoke design that greatly resembled those from the Mach III concept car from 1993. The horizontal three-bar taillamp motif became a vertical three-bar taillight motif, in better keeping with Mustang tradition (the lamps themselves were made of a jewel-like plastic that was itself very attractive). A honeycomb grille insert reminiscent of the 1971–1973 Mach 1 Mustangs filled the opening in the front fascia, but it

hindered cooling, especially on the Cobra, and was gone by 1997.

Badges proclaiming "4.6L GT" adorned the front fenders, and the interior changes included a switch from two-tone interiors to monochrome units. New colors included bright tangerine, pacific green, and moonlight blue metallic. (Bright tangerine turned out to be a one-year/GT-only color.)

Predictably, sales of the Cobra were brisk (despite its $25,000-plus sticker price), while GT sales fell drastically. Overall production declined in '96 and '97, which Ford attributed to the softening of the ponycar market in general. Many believe that the downturn in sales is due to the high price and poor performance of the GT. Only three years earlier, a buyer could purchase a $15,000 LX that would run the tires off almost any new car; to get equal performance now, you had to opt for one of the Cobras, most of which came fully equipped at a sticker price of more than $27,000 for a coupe and nearly $30,000 for a convertible.

The GT was perceived in the high-performance market as a nonplayer—a very nice, competent car,

but hardly the tire fryer it had once been. With prices creeping into the $23,000 range for a nicely equipped 4.6 GT, a lot of potential customers either kept their 5.0s or switched to Camaros and Firebirds, which now sported 285-horsepower 350s (305 horsepower in SS or Ram Air trim). In an attempt to lure budget-conscious buyers back to the showrooms, Ford reincarnated the GTS, although it wasn't called that. Again, the company did nothing to trumpet the model's return and most dealers had no idea how to order one. Those in the know ordered Package 248A, which deleted the power group, fog lights, rear wing, and more. Few were built and Ford canceled it in 1998. (To its credit, Ford made more options standard at a better price in '98, but those looking for a bare-bones ponycar were out of luck.)

For 1998, the Mustang GT received a 10-horsepower boost, but once again it was basically a carryover vehicle.

As of this writing, major changes are in store for 1999. The Mustang GT has received a boost to 260 horsepower, while the Cobra will benefit from new cylinder heads, a different intake manifold, and a 15-hp increase. Independent rear suspension has become standard.

The Fox-4 platform is also expected to see its first (and more than likely last) major face-lift. Slightly flared fenders, a different front fascia, a new tail treatment, and a more aggressive overall appearance are part of the package.

The most tantalizing rumors, though, revolve around the possibility of a '99 or 2000 Cobra R. This powerhouse is expected to receive a four-valve-per-cylinder 5.4-liter DOHC engine making upward of 400 horsepower. Other reports touch on the possibility of an independent rear suspension, six-speed manual transmission, enormous brakes, and perhaps even a short-/long-arm (SLA) front suspension.

The drawback to all these goodies is that the vehicle would likely cost upward of $50,000, and again, availability would be severely limited. If it were built, it would certainly be the most outrageous, fastest, best-handling Mustang ever.

THE END OF
THE FOX LINE

More than likely, the Fox-4 Mustang will be gone by the year 2001, 2002 at the latest. Its replacement is said to be coming on the DEW–98 rear-wheel-drive platform, upon which Ford will base a host of new rear-drive vehicles, including the next-generation Thunderbird and certain Jaguar models. Ford is said to be committed to the Mustang at least until 2005, and it will certainly soldier on with a V8 engine sending power south to the differential via a driveshaft. That's wonderful news for performance fans everywhere.

And there's no doubt that when this new pony is foaled, it will be a remarkable and revolutionary piece of equipment, endowed with the spirit of almost forty years of unbridled Mustang mania. When the next generation arrives, it will signal the end of the Fox Mustang era, which, implausibly, will have lasted nearly twenty-five years.

Will it be as successful as the Fox and Fox-4 Mustangs? Only time will tell, and even then it depends on your definition of success. We can only speculate on whether it will be smaller or larger, faster or slower—though we will go out on a limb and say it will certainly be more expensive.

Though the Fox platform had its faults, its production life will have lasted almost a quarter century. That's an eternity for a modern automobile. (By comparison, depending on when the last Fox car is built, it may have been in production longer than the Model T!)

With any luck, the next generation of Mustangs will create the same kind of sensation and inspire the same type of devotion and fanaticism as the fabulous Foxes of the past twenty years. Despite its humble roots, the Fox Mustang will be a tough act to follow.

Opposite: Drawing heavily from Mustangs of the 1960s, as well as the "Rambo" concept car, the '99 Mustang received a controversial body makeover. Hood and side scoops are non-functional. This one has the optional 17-inch (43.2cm) wheels. **Above:** By contrast, the 1994–1998 Mustangs had more conventional styling. This GT has the standard 16-inch (40.6cm) wheels and Firestone tires.

6 | SVT Mustang
Power, Prestige & Performance

Back in the '60s, the ultimate Mustangs and Fords wore the coiled snake emblem first seen on Carroll Shelby's magnificent Cobra race cars. Powered by Ford's small-block and big-block V8 engines, the Cobras captured road racing and drag racing championships around the world, setting numerous records in the process. As the decade wore on, Shelby worked his magic on the 1965 Mustang, creating the GT350. Eventually, Ford attached the Cobra name to its most fearsome power plants and muscle cars, including the 428 Cobra Jet (and Super Cobra Jet), the 351 Cobra Jet, the Torino Cobra, and the Mustang Cobra.

The Cobra nomenclature would be shelved for a time after 1973, only to reappear on the top-of-the-line 1979 Mustang models. It continued on for three years, but when the 5.0 H.O. engine appeared in '82, the snake again took a rest, making way for the heralded GT.

When Ford formed the Special Vehicle Team in 1990 to build and create unique, high-performance automobiles, it revived the glory of the Cobra name on the Mustang, and unlike in the late 1970s and early 1980s, this time the cars truly earned their fangs. In every sense, the 1993–present Mustang Cobras are thrilling rides.

Ford SVT's mission was similar to that of the defunct Special Vehicle Operations group of the 1980s, that being to produce limited-production, high-zoot variations of regular assembly line cars. But, as discussed in chapter three, SVO never really got off the ground; the only car it ever brought to market was the ill-fated Mustang SVO. Not wanting a repeat performance, Ford were careful in developing the SVT division.

The goal of SVT was to build cars (and trucks, as it turned out) that stood apart from mainstream products—machines that had improved acceleration, ride, handling, control, brakes, and appearance. In the case of the Mustang, SVT had to refine "those virtues inherent to

every V8-powered Mustang: a favorable power-to-weight ratio and the responsive handling characteristics exclusive to a front-engine, rear-drive chassis layout," according to Ford's original press releases.

The goals didn't end with the cars, however. Ford was trying to create a new atmosphere for the customers of these vehicles as well (in part because, like the SVO, cars wearing the SVT badge would be quite a bit more expensive than their standard showroom counterparts). Not every Ford dealer would be selling the Cobra and its sister ship, the F-150 Lightning truck: these would be available only through SVT dealerships. To become one, a franchise would have to pay a fee, and then members of its sales staff and service department would be specially trained about SVT products. Initially, less than 25 percent of Ford's dealerships opted to become SVT outlets and some dropped out after the first year. Today, the total number of SVT dealers is around 720. The result is a better-trained sales and service force that, while not perfect, is more often than not a cut above.

One of the original members of Ford's Special Vehicle Team was Neil Ressler, at the time its Executive Director, Vehicle Engineering, and the Executive Director (Cobra). Said Ressler, by 1997 the Vice President, Advanced Vehicle Technology, Ford Automotive Operations, "Our original vision for SVT was to have cars that represent a balance between sophistication and competent vehicle dynamics, the kind of car enthusiasts would enjoy driving."

Obviously, by 1993 the original Fox Mustang was getting old and, despite increases in performance, somewhat stale. It was a perfect opportunity for Ford's new team to show the automotive world just what SVT was all about. Among the Mustang's flaws were a somewhat harsh ride, handling that was just so-so, braking that was below average, and an appearance that was fine but at that point in its seventh model year. Ford SVT took on all of these problems, and the result of their work was the quickest, smoothest, best-braking Fox Mustang to that point—the perfect machine to end a long, brilliant run.

All SVT Cobras in '93 were built on the hatchback body with the GT's air dam. To freshen the car's appearance, it was infused with special touches. Unique rocker moldings were added to the sides, a salami-slicer rear wing was fitted to the decklid, and an opening was cut into the grille replete with a galloping horse emblem (a hint of what was to come on the '94 Mustang).

In a first for a Fox Mustang, special 17- by 7.5-inch (43.1 by 19cm) directional wheels were employed, wrapped in Goodyear Eagle (P245/45ZR17) tires. They aided greatly in handling (according to *Motor Trend*, the Cobra was capable of .86 g on the skidpad) and gave the car a distinctive, high-dollar appearance.

Spring rates, anti–roll bar diameters, shock absorber characteristics, and suspension mounting bushings were all tuned to achieve a balance between a more supple ride and optimum handling and response. While the front springs were the same progressive-rate pieces used in the GT/LX 5.0s, the rears used linear-rate and significantly softer (160 pounds-inches vs. 200 to 300 pounds-inches) springs for a better ride.

Ford then employed specially tuned shocks and struts to dial in the suspension. A smaller front sway bar was installed, while the same rear bar that was used on all '87 and later 5-liter Stangs was fitted out back.

The resultant suspension had loads of grip, but it confounded those used to the punishing ride characteristics of traditional muscle cars. Body roll was more pronounced and the seats didn't do a tremendous job of holding the driver in place. It felt less confidence-inspiring, yet actual testing showed it to be very capable. And unlike the GT and LX, it was especially smooth around town and on long journeys—exactly what SVT was hoping for.

The SVT Cobra was the first Mustang since the '86 SVO to use four-wheel disc brakes. They measured 10.84 inches (27.5cm) up front and 10.07 inches (25.5cm) out back and could knock almost 20 feet (6m) off a 60-to-0-mph (96.5 to 0kph) braking distance, a huge improvement. Equally (if not more) important, they were fade-resistant and could bring the car down from speed repeatedly.

This was very good news because the '93 Cobra could really haul asp. Ford made numerous improvements to the 5.0's intake tract and the result was significantly more ponies. Interestingly, Ford rated the Cobra at 235 horsepower—30 more than the '93 GT but just 10 more than the 1987–1992 cars. In the press kit for the media's first drive of the SVT Cobra and Lightning, no numbers were set, but it noted that "preliminary estimates indicate an increase of about 40 horsepower over the current 5.0 power plant."

Ford used a version of the iron GT-40 cylinder heads, a cast version of the SVO GT-40 intake manifold, and 1.72 rocker arms (to give the cam more lift). The heads offered numerous improvements over stock, including larger intake and exhaust ports and bigger intake and exhaust valves. A 70mm mass air meter and 65mm throttle body let the air into the engine, where it was fed by 24-pound-per-hour fuel injectors (19-pound-per-hour injectors were used on the 5.0 H.O.).

The strangest part used was the camshaft, which was out of the Thunderbird's 5.0. Because of the special intake tract, low-end torque was down somewhat. The T-Bird cam remedied this situation at the expense of top-end horsepower.

Whatever the actual rating, the '93 Cobra was the quickest Fox Mustang yet. And it appeared not a moment too soon because around the same time it landed at dealer showrooms, Chevrolet's swoopy new Camaro Z/28 was introduced. The Mustang-Camaro rivalry had never been hotter, though the Mustang had enjoyed a performance advantage for the better part of ten years. Chevy fans felt they finally had something to crow about in the Z/28, which had 275 horsepower, a six-speed transmission, and four-wheel disc brakes (with an antilock system), not to mention space-age styling and inspired handling. No, the Cobra arrived not a moment too soon.

In the first direct comparison of the two cars, *Muscle Mustangs & Fast Fords* brought them together at Old Bridge Township Raceway Park in Englishtown, New Jersey, for its July 1993 issue. To level the playing field, the Camaro was driven by members of *Vette* magazine, a sister publication. When the tire smoke cleared, the

Cobra emerged victorious in straightline competition, running a 13.75 at 98.27 mph (158.1kph) to the Z/28's 13.88 at 99.19 mph (159.5kph). The Camaro succumbed to a tank of bad fuel later in the test. Still, with the "10-minute tune-up," the Cobra ran a smoldering 13.47 at 100.81 mph (162.2kph), making it the quickest damn Mustang since the 428 Cobra Jets of the '60s.

Best of all, it wasn't just a straightline rocket ship. Oh, the engine was plenty willing in every situation, but

Pages 76–77: The '94 Cobra was unveiled to the media at Bob Bondurant's driving school in Chandler, Arizona. **Opposite:** The SVT Lightning had a GT-40-sized 351 with enough power to propel the 4,600-pound (1,716kg) truck to low-15-second quarter-mile times. **Above, top:** Shortly after the Lightning and Cobra hit the market, the Cobra R was released in very limited quantities. **Above, bottom:** The 275-horsepower Camaro Z/28 was all-new for '93 and was serious competition for the 235-horsepower Cobra.

the suspension did not beat you up and the brakes were a massive improvement. Ford had no trouble finding homes for the 4,993 it produced between August 4, 1992, and June 28, 1993. According to Robert Lyons of the SVT Cobra Owners Association, Cobra number 19 was the first released to the general public and was assembled on December 17, 1992.

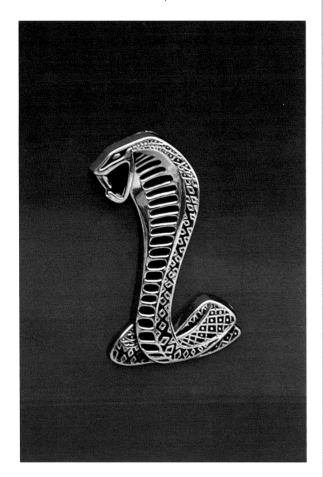

MODERN ASP-IRATIONS

With all the hoopla that surrounded the introduction of the Fox-4 Mustang in 1994, there was grave disappointment among the faithful because the standard 5.0 engine produced a mere 215 horsepower, 60 shy of the hot LT1 Camaros and Firebirds. It was not long, however, before Ford's Special Vehicle Team answered the call. Although the new Cobra didn't have the 275-plus-horsepower engine enthusiasts wanted, it did have an underrated 240-hp version of the GT-40-ized 5-liter— basically a carryover engine from the '93 with the exception of the 90-degree elbow for the throttle body endemic to all V8 SN95 Mustangs. Ford also threw in

"R" MEANS RACE: THE 1993 SVT COBRA R

For the first time since Shelby built his race-ready GT350 R models, Ford offered a road course–ready rocket through its dealer body. Based on the '93 Cobra, it was also called the Cobra R, and as always, "R" meant race.

Ford's Special Vehicle Engineering group designed the car to be competitive in the "showroom stock" ranks of SCCA and IMSA road racing series. Though their drivetrains were identical, there were vast differences between the Cobra and Cobra R. For starters, the radio and rear seat were deleted in the R model, as were all the sound-deadening material, the inner fender panels, the fog lights, and the rear defroster. Air conditioning was not an option, but power steering and power brakes remained. Even the seats were of the low-back, SSP variety, which saved close to 20 pounds (9kg).

All 107 R models produced were painted vibrant red and fitted with opal gray cloth front seats. Rolling stock consisted of P245/45ZR17 Goodyear "gatorback" Eagle tires and unique 17- by 8-inch (43.1 by 20.3cm) five-lug wheels that were painted black with chrome center caps. (These wheels, in unpainted, clearcoat form, would become optional on the 1994 Mustang GT.) Unlike production Cobras, a full-size spare with a matching wheel came in the trunk.

To prepare the cars for the rigors of racing, four-wheel disc brakes were standard, but the fronts were upgraded to 13.5-inch (34.2cm) rotors with twin-piston PBR calipers, the rears to 11.65 inches (29.5cm). Heavy-duty Koni shocks and struts were standard, the front and rear springs were stiffened, the front sway bar was fattened, and a strut tower brace tied the fenders and the cowl together. Ford also reinforced the floor pan and rocker panels and provided additional chassis bracing.

The stock radiator was replaced with a heavy-duty aluminum unit, and there was also an engine oil cooler and a power steering fluid cooler. Semifinished Cobra Rs were shipped from the Dearborn assembly plant to Creative Industries in Detroit, where final assembly was handled.

These were not inexpensive automobiles. The price was $25,217, and many sold for above sticker. Ford also made purchasers sign a waiver stating that they understood the Cobra R was built for racing, which released Ford from the liabilities of the dangers of racing. Prospective buyers had to have a competition license from one of the major race-sanctioning bodies like the SCCA or the NHRA in order to purchase the cars, and they had to agree to race them in competition.

Few Cobra Rs saw actual race duty; many ended up in car collections and never turned a tire in battle. Still, some people did race the R, though with little success. Among the problems was a lack of proper on-track development time. Also, the fuel tank was the same 15.4-gallon (58.2L) unit common to all Stangs. That meant frequent pit stops for fuel, a major drawback during a long-endurance race. But despite its lack of racing success, the '93 R is one of the rarest and most desirable Fox Mustangs. It was an instant collectible.

an oil cooler, a lighter flywheel, and a redesigned alternator pulley for a couple of extra horsepower. The factory rating was 240 hp at 4800 rpm and 285 pounds-feet of torque at 4000.

(Generally speaking, the addition of the GT-40 equipment, larger throttle body, and mass air meter on a 5.0 H.O. is worth approximately 60 horsepower, which means that the production Cobras were putting out closer to 275 horsepower even if they were rated far lower.)

The cars were introduced to the media at the Bob Bondurant School of High Performance Driving outside Phoenix, Arizona. There, journalists were treated to a tech session, a walk around the cars, and then hours of laps on the twisty, challenging road course. From the minute you buckled yourself into the cockpit, it became readily apparent that this was no ordinary Mustang.

While the '94 Cobra shared the refinement inherent to all SN95 Mustangs, it burned up the track at

Bondurant's. Helping to improve handling were pretty 17- by 8-inch (43.1 by 20.3cm) wheels with Goodyear P255/45ZR Eagle GS-C tires, at the time Goodyear's best. Instead of the GT's variable-rate springs, the linear-rate coils from the six-cylinder Mustang were substituted for a softer ride. A thinner-diameter front sway bar (25mm vs. 30mm) and a thicker rear one (27mm vs. 24mm) altered handling.

As was the case with the '93 Cobra, body roll was more apparent, though the car felt a bit more neutral. What truly differentiated the Cobra from the GT was the stampede of extra ponies under the hood. They woke the car up and made it a blast to drive.

Making the whole vehicle safer were the brakes, pirated from the '93 R model—13-inch (33cm) rotors, dual-piston PBR calipers up front, 11.65-inch (29.5cm) rotors in the rear. Better still, ABS was standard.

In addition to the wheels, helping to improve the visual statement were a different front fascia with round

Opposite: In 1993, the coiled snake emblem appeared on a Mustang for the first time since 1978. This time, it was on a powerful performance car, not a pretender. **Below:** Ford's Special Vehicle Team began marketing the Mustang Cobra in 1993. Except for an obscure Canada-only option package in the mid-1980s, Ford had not used the hallowed Cobra name on a Mustang since the less-than-deserving 1981 model.

fog lights and compound reflector headlamps, a Cobra-only wing that housed a trick LED center high-mounted stop light (base and GT Mustangs had the CHMSL located in the trunk lid above the license plate), and coiled snake emblems on the front fenders where the GT badges had been. You could get any color you wanted as long as it was crystal white, black, or Rio red.

The only enhancement to the interior was the soon-to-be traditional SVT white-face gauge cluster with a 160-mph (257.4kph) speedometer and 7000-rpm tach with a 5800-rpm redline. As with the '93 Cobra, this was the biggest disappointment of the whole car. Back in '84, the SVO was introduced with excellent multi-adjustable, articulated seats, repositioned pedals, and a host of handsome touches. Despite its robust sticker price (coupes started at $20,765 and most sold for about $24,020), the Cobra shared 99 percent of its office with the run-of-the-mill GT. Every Cobra built used a T-5 five-speed transmission with phosphate-coated gears for improved durability.

When the Cobra was unleashed, it was announced that there would now be a convertible model, too. This was cause for celebration, as there hadn't been a serpentine ragtop since the 1969–1970 Shelby Mustangs. Plans called for one thousand to be built and all would be Indianapolis Pace Car replicas. That's correct: a Cobra would be pacing the seventy-eighth big race at the Brickyard. Ford did indeed produce one thousand Pace Cars, all rio red clearcoat with saddle leather interiors. The Pace Cars differed in that the openings of the spokes in their wheels were painted charcoal instead of being left unpainted, and a plethora of Indianapolis Pace Car decals were included, to be owner- or dealer-installed. Prices were $20,765 for the coupe, $23,535 for the droptop.

This author was present when the Cobras were introduced at Bondurant, and tested a '94 Cobra for *Muscle Mustangs & Fast Fords*. Both days offered weather that could make the devil himself sweat, but it was plain to see that the new breed of snake was the best yet. The car pulled .86 g on the skidpad, accelerated to 60 mph (96.5kph) in 5.7 seconds, and hit 140 mph (225.2kph).

When drag tested, the car ran a 14.29 at 96.98 mph (156kph) despite 97°F (36°C) ambient temps. With a little finagling, the car lit up the scoreboards with a 13.87 at 99.49 mph (160kph); the thermometer read an even 100°F (38°C) when that occurred. In cooler weather, the car would no doubt have gone a few tenths of a second quicker, making it nearly as potent as the lighter, less refined '93.

The SN95-based Cobra was a sweetheart of a deal, but the 5-liter engine's days were winding down. The car was a carryover for '95, the last year for the Windsor engine in the Fox Mustang, and many decided to get a hi-po 5.0 before the more complex modular V8 arrived. Actual production slipped to 4,005 coupes and 1,003 convertibles, but that doesn't tell the entire story for '95. Ford finally produced a 5.8L Cobra, and while it limited output to 250 units, they were the most memorable Fox Mustangs ever. With black paint and a gorgeous saddle tan interior, this Cobra turned heads wherever it went.

Below: For the first time since 1979, the Mustang was selected as the official Pace Car for the Indianapolis 500. All Cobra convertibles in '94 were rio red/saddle leather Indy Pace Car replicas.

Above: One of the rarest Mustang options was the hardtop for the '95 Cobra convertible. Originally intended as an option for all SN95 ragtops, it was available for one year only and just on the Cobra. All '95 Cobra convertibles were black. **Inset:** 1995 was the last hurrah for the 5.0 engine in a Mustang; the next year all Cobras would receive 4.6L dual-overhead-cam V8s.

WHITE LIGHTNING: THE 1995 COBRA R

Every inch of the beast bristled with muscle. The hood bulged to accommodate the new, larger engine and was open at the rear to reduce heat in the engine compartment. The tires were fat BFGoodrich Comp T/A radials on sinewy five-spoke alloys, prettier yet more aggressive than any wheel the factory had previously used. Viewed from behind, a 20-gallon (75.7L) fuel cell was visible; it hung below the rear bumper cover, giving the car "balls."

Perhaps more than anything else, the cell was symbolic of how far Ford was pushing the envelope. This was a take-no-prisoners warrior, street-legal, but not for the faint of heart.

It was lower, meaner, and (best of all) faster than any Mustang ever made—quicker than the Cobra Jets, GT500s, Boss 429s, all of them. It was the 1995 R model Cobra.

Each was identical: refrigerator white with tan cloth seats from the six-cylinder Mustang. Pulse-raising pleasure in a plain wrapper.

Like their 1993 counterparts, the '95 Cobra Rs were built to homologate the model for SCCA and IMSA road racing (and to a far lesser degree NHRA and IHRA drag racing). When the '93 Rs got stomped in competition, Ford learned the hard way what it needed to make them competitive and applied that knowledge to the '95.

To wit, the stock 15.4-gallon (58.2L) gas tank was too small. Ergo, a 20-gallon (75.7L) fuel cell replaced it. Yes, a regular 20-gallon (75.7L) street-car gas tank could have been fitted, but these were going to be race cars, so why bother?

Yes, the GT-40-enhanced 5.0 was strong, but it was at a 48-cubic-inch disadvantage to the 350 small-block Chevy in the Camaros and Firebirds. Presto, a 351 (or 5.8L) Windsor replete with all the "good stuff"—cylinder heads, intake, headers, and more—was stuffed under the bonnet.

As with the '93, all superfluous, nonessential goodies were pitched. That meant no radio, no sound deadeners, no rear seat, no rear defroster, no air conditioner, no power windows—no kidding. These deletions helped offset the extra weight of the larger engine, though the car weighs 154 pounds (69.9kg) more than a "regular" Cobra.

Ah, yes, the engine. Ford said it was a hybrid, based on the 351 marine engine and built at the Windsor, Ontario, plant. It had a 9:1 compression ratio, GT-40 heads, cast Cobra intake, SVO valve train, and 80mm mass air meter. All used an engine oil cooler, a water-to-oil power steering cooler, and specially calibrated EEC-IV engine computer. Originally, it was said to make 280 horsepower, but when tested every engine made at least 300 horses so that is what the rating was (at 4800 rpm), and 365 pounds-feet of torque at 3750 rpm.

Backing this up was a Tremec five-speed transmission, a heavy-duty 10.5-inch (26.6cm) SVO clutch, a shortened driveshaft, and 3.27:1 Traction-Lok rear.

Adjustable Koni struts and shocks sat at the appropriate corners and progressive-rate Eibach springs were installed—700- to 850-pound-per-inch coils in front and 200- to 260-pound coils out back. A fat 30mm sway bar was installed up front (vs. 25mm on a regular Cobra) and a 27mm bar was in the rear (same as stock). Rolling stock consisted of 17- by 9-inch (43.1 by 22.8cm) A-Mold wheels all around and P255/45ZR tires.

The fog lights were omitted again, to duct fresh air to the front brakes.

The 252 R models began life on the regular Mustang line at the Dearborn assembly plant but were shipped minus hoods, cooling systems, and fuel tanks to Masco Tech in Detroit for final assembly. The hoods were painted at Masco (the regular paint ovens in Dearborn were too hot for fiberglass), and the heavy-duty aluminum radiators and Fuel-Safe fuel cells were added. Finally the hoods were bolted in place and the cars were inspected by DAP personnel and shipped to the appropriate SVT dealers.

The same rules of purchase applied to the '95 R models that applied to the '93s (competition license, waiver, and so on), and like the earlier cars, the '95s were completely street-legal automobiles—though hardly practical.

Yes, many ended up in the hands of collectors and a few were even registered for street use, but this time many ended up in fender-to-fender competition. The Steeda Autosports Cobra R racked up the model's first victory at Texas World Speedway in 1995 in IMSA Grand Sport competition (and in the process became the first Ford to ever win a GS race). Steeda had

Because of the car's deep-skirted block design, Ford had to reconfigure the Mustang's K-member and suspension geometry. While they were at it, Ford's suspension gurus hacked around with spring rates and shocks, the result of which was a much more neutral-handling Cobra. Gone were the linear-rate springs in favor of 400- to 505-pounds-inch progressive coils (front) and 165- to 265-pounds-inch pieces (rear). The shocks and struts were revalved, and the front sway bar was fattened to 29mm.

For the first time, BFGoodrich Comp T/As were standard equipment on a non-R model Cobra. They measured P245/45ZR17 all around, and one of the reasons for the switch from Goodyear GS-Cs was how impressed Ford was with the tires from their testing with the '95 R.

Like all non-R Cobras, the '96 and later versions rode about 1½ inches (3.8cm) too high off the ground, and they seemed as if they were standing on their toes. This was a fine-handling car, but it just didn't look the part. Again, the goal was a smooth ride, neutral balance, and plenty of stick.

From a looks standpoint, the Cobra received the same basic appearance enhancements as the rest of the Mustang lineup, including vertical three-bar taillamps and a honeycomb grille insert. The Cobra was the sole recipient of a domed hood that featured a pair of fake air scoops. Color choices were revised a bit. Black and white returned, but Rio red was gone, replaced by laser red tinted clearcoat metallic, a very popular color on the GT. There was also a special-order paint, mystic, which changed colors from black to metallic green to maroon to gold depending upon how the light hit it. It was an expensive proposition at $815, and only 1,999 were built, all with black interiors.

From a performance standpoint, the 4.6 Cobra was clearly quicker than the 5.0 Cobra it replaced. Though the mainstream automotive press had a difficult time posting sub-14-second quarter-mile (402.3m) times, the enthusiast press didn't, for the most part. *Drag Racing Monthly*, in an all-out shootout with the '96 Camaro SS, stomped the Chevy with a 13.48 at 101.7 mph (163.6kph). *Muscle Mustangs & Fast Fords'* first test (with slicks, no less) was a 13.62 at 99 mph

(159.2kph). A second (with a mystic Cobra) resulted in a 13.31.

Impressive, yes, but not the quickest ever. Still, the four-valve-per-cylinder snake cannot be judged by mere quarter-mile (402.3m) numbers or by its top speed of 154 mph (247.7kph). It is the most sophisticated and refined ponycar to date, full of technology, performance, and smoothness.

"The Cobra's transient handling proves more than a match for any sports coupe on the market. Not only can you position the nose with the throttle, [but] even crossing back and forth over the ragged edge of traction sends linear controllable messages through the seat," raved *Sports Car International* magazine in its June/July 1996 issue. It went on, "The 1996 Cobra is not only the best Mustang ever, it's far and away the sweetest V8 sports coupe you can buy for the money. It looks and feels comparatively sedate, but it is also heart-stoppingly fast and incredibly competent when taken flat-out."

Cooling system upgrades and exterior color changes marked the next two years of Cobra production. Laser red would be replaced by Rio red in '97, only to come back in '98, and in doing so made rio red a one-year color choice for modular Cobras. Other '98 hues would be white, black, bright yellow, Pacific green, and bright Atlantic blue. True to its word, Ford kept mystic as a one-year-only option, and though it bounced around the idea of doing another flip-flop-type paint, it has yet to do so.

Rumors flew around about the '99 Cobra, and while a 5.4 four-valve R model is considered a "done deal," the Mustang world waits for a similarly powered, fully optioned street model for the masses. If such a car were to appear before the Fox-4 platform ceases production, it could be the first 12-second factory "street" Stang.

Note: A breakdown of production numbers and color combinations for the 1993–1997 SVT Cobras is available in the appendix at the back of this book.

7

Foxier Foxes
The Ultra Stangs

 **Exploding across the desert in 1996 at 177 mph (284.7kph) is the fastest of all Mustangs. Even at these highly illegal speeds, the car is glued to the pavement. At nearly three times the posted speed limit, the car feels as stable as if you were traveling at 65 mph (104.5kph) on the way to the beach. The car has a race-bred suspension, giant brakes, and enough air dams and spoilers to keep you from getting airborne. It is a supercharged Saleen S-351 Mustang.**

Throughout the history of the automobile, there have been people and companies that have refused to settle for the performance or styling delivered to them by the factory. Since day one, custom coach builders installed different bodies on existing production vehicles. In the '60s, men like Don Yenko, Bob Tasca, and Joel Rosen took America's muscle cars and transformed them into land-based missiles with engines much bigger and more powerful than the factory would provide.

In the 1970s and early 1980s, domestic and European firms scrambled to provide the kind of handling and speed not available from showroom-stock cars. The Fox Mustang could no sooner escape this trend than any other performance automobile. Its low price, solid foundation, and adaptable mechanicals made it a natural. Some of these creations had beefed-up suspensions; others added horsepower and/or styling; few had all three. One thing all their creators had was a desire to develop the ultimate Mustang, one better than stock at a price that was commensurate with such performance and exclusivity.

Not all of these attempts were successful. Some, in fact, were miserable failures. Others had (and have) the blessing of Ford Motor Company. The one thing they shared was that to one degree or another, they were all interesting.

ASC/McLAREN CAPRIS & MUSTANGS

One of the first attempts at factory one-upmanship was the ASC/McLaren Mustang.

Engineer Peter Muscat got the idea for it when his wife, a Ford employee, complained that she was not permitted to park her car of choice, a Mercedes SL roadster, closer to her office. One of the inspirations for the styling on the '79 Fox Mustang coupe was this very Mercedes. His wife liked convertibles, but in 1982, the Mustang was available only as a hatchback or coupe. An engineer by trade, Muscat purchased a 1980 Mustang coupe and produced his own version of the Mercedes roadster, complete with a two-seat configuration and a top that folded completely out of sight under a hard cover.

Muscat presented the car to Ford officials, who were impressed with his concept and execution, but not his timing. Ford, it turned out, was just about to introduce the 1983 Mustang convertible, the first ragtop in the lineup in ten years. It didn't need another. Mercury, however, was not slated to get such a model for the Capri, and sales of the Mustang's sister car had been slipping a bit. The marriage was a natural. Ford contracted the American Sunroof Corporation (ASC) to build the cars under its Automotive Specialty Corporation and then return them to Ford for shipment.

What was the McLaren connection? McLaren, famous worldwide for its racing exploits, provided the custom spring rates, Carrera shocks and struts, and trick wheels. Unfortunately, it did not provide any engine modifications.

For three years (beginning in 1984), Mercury sold these creations (see sidebar on page 97 for sales figures), with its creator getting $500 per car. At the time of its introduction, the ASC/McLaren Capri cost some $21,000, a startling sum for a ponycar. When the Capri was discontinued after the 1986 model year, ASC/McLaren production was switched over to the Mustang, where it continued until 1990. The Mustangs all started life as LX coupes but were built with GT noses. Ford actually gave the car a small advertising

budget to promote sales. By this point, the price of the ASC/McLaren had risen to nearly $25,000 (all were convertibles).

The best year for this special Fox chassis product was 1988, when sales exploded, breaking the 1,000 unit plateau. Among its standard features were leather seats, steering wheel and shift knob, a unique console, premium sound system, lowering springs, and 15 by 7-inch McLaren wheels.

In spite of the sales success of '88, a licensing disagreement between Muscat and ASC resulted in a shortage of cars. Production plummeted over the next two years, and the car was discontinued at the end of the model year. Although these were very interesting cars and they sold surprisingly well, they have become little-remembered footnotes in the Fox chassis' history.

Preceding pages: A 1989 white SSC from Saleen. **Above:** Ford took some of its styling cues for the '79 Mustang from the 450SL Mercedes. This roadster became the inspiration for the ASC/McLaren Capris and Mustangs of 1983–1990. **Opposite:** After the Capri ceased production in 1986, ASC/McLaren turned its attention to the Fox Mustang. **Opposite, inset:** One nice touch on the ASC/McLaren Mustangs was custom embroidered headrests.

ASC/McLAREN PRODUCTION

Year	Totals
1984	60
1985	405
1986	407
1987	479
1988	1,015
1989	247
1990	65

Note: Of the 874 cars produced from 1984 to 1986, all were Capris except for six Mustang prototypes.

SALEEN MUSTANGS

The most successful of all ultra Stangs has been the Saleen Mustang. Created by southern California road racer Steve Saleen, it is different from all the other cars in this chapter (except for the ASC McLaren) because it is a Ford-authorized vehicle that comes with a factory warranty (as well as a Saleen warranty). Furthermore, Saleen Performance is a small-volume vehicle manufacturer, meaning its cars are certified by the federal Environmental Protection Agency (EPA) and the California Air Resources Board (CARB) for sale in all fifty states.

As such, Saleen Mustangs must pass rigorous tests and meet exacting standards. Only those parts certified for use may be installed. The other cars to be mentioned are commonly called "tuner" cars, which are modified by a company, often to a customer's whim, and may be sold through specific dealers but usually are not covered by all warranties or certified by the EPA and CARB.

Saleen first approached Ford with his proposition for the Saleen Mustang in November 1983. He got Ford's blessing in February 1984, and in June of that year he introduced the first Saleen Mustang at Sears Point Raceway in Sonoma, California, at a Trans-Am race in which he was competing. That first car, assigned serial number 32 to give the media the impression that more cars were built than actually had been, was actually owned by Saleen's sister Robin. In fact, only three Saleen Mustangs—all LX-based hatchbacks—were built in '84. It was a slow start but one that would gather momentum in short order. (Saleen was kind enough to return the first car to his sister when he had finished with it.)

Above: The first year for Saleen Mustang production was 1984. Only three were produced, including the prototype, which was owned by Steve Saleen's sister.

Although it was impressive to look at, the 170-mph (273.5kph) speedometer was quite unnecessary. To keep the car's factory warranty in effect, the engine remained stock (though there was a chrome air cleaner lid with a Saleen graphic).

The result was a very exciting car, one that handled capably but sacrificed any semblance of ride quality. In fact, this would be a Saleen trait until the all-new '94 models debuted. Few cared, though. Ford fans, desperate for a race-bred Mustang since the '66 Shelby GT350, embraced both the car and the concept. And back in '84, the prevailing logic was that cars that handled had to have rock-hard suspensions. It was a trade-off worn like a badge of honor.

Changes were few for '85. Ford had increased horsepower to 210, a definite step in the right direction. Saleen added better brake pads to the front discs for improved stopping, and there was a subtle running change with the front air dam, thanks to a switch in vendors. Production increased to 139 hatchbacks and two convertibles, but it could be a struggle to find a dealer who actually knew what a Saleen was or how to order one.

Production went up again in '86, to 187 hatchbacks and twelve convertibles, and there were further refinements to the interior and exterior, but it wasn't until the 225-horsepower 5-liter H.O. engine was installed in all 1987 V8 Mustangs that the Saleens took off. Production increased to 278 in '87 and hit 708 and 891 in the two years following. Included in those totals for the first time were a number of coupes. The first (and only one built in 1987) went to Austin Craig, a J. Walter Thompson Advertising executive who handled the Ford Motorsport account. The car looked especially tough and production would continue into 1990, but Saleen customers were more interested in hatchbacks and convertibles. In four years, total coupe production was just fifty-three cars.

A special model, the Saleen SSC, was introduced in 1989. For the first time, a Saleen had an engine that was substantially different from the factory Ford power plant. Also revised from the standard Saleen Mustang was the appearance. All were white with yellow and

At $14,300, the Saleen Mustang was not cheap, but there were enough upgrades to justify the price. The car was lowered on special Racecraft springs, Bilstein gas-pressurized shocks and struts were used, and urethane bushings replaced the stock rubber pieces for improved performance. A chassis brace was added, and the car rolled on Goodyear P215/60HR15 Eagle GT tires and Hayashi wheels. The front-end alignment was also altered for better tracking and response.

To differentiate the Saleens from stock Mustangs (and at the same time improve aerodynamics), the cars were fitted with a unique front air dam, rear spoiler, side skirts, and spats. Tricolor stripes adorned the sides, and clear headlight covers smoothed the air at the front of the vehicle. The side window louvers were painted to match the body.

Inside, a 170-mph (273.5kph) speedometer greeted the driver, mounted in the factory location behind a custom four-spoke steering wheel. A Saleen shift knob was screwed onto the shifter, and special plaques (including one that serialized the vehicle) adorned the dash and console. The Saleen logo was etched to the speedometer and tach. Also standard were an Escort radar detector and an alarm system.

black chevrons that started on the front fenders and finished on the doors. Unique white-painted wheels and custom two-tone leather Flofit seats were also part of the package. Most unusual was that the car was assembled as a two-seater. The rear seat was removed and the area carpeted.

Saleen was claiming about 300 horsepower for the SSC's 5-liter engine and a top speed of 156 mph (251kph). The changes included a set of ported stock cylinder heads, a larger throttle body, larger-diameter ceramic-coated tube headers with a Dynomax cat-back exhaust system, modified upper and lower intake manifolds, and 1.7:1 rocker arms. When all was said and done, the most oft-quoted power figure is 290 horses. Helping to get the package moving was a 3.55:1 rear gear and an Auburn differential.

Keeping it in line were four-wheel disc brakes with special grooved rotors, five-lug wheels, Monroe Formula GP cockpit-adjustable shocks and struts, and SSC-only wheels with General XP2000 Z-rated tires.

At $36,500, the SSC was a very expensive proposition—for the same money, you could buy three 5-liter LXs and get change. But this car struck a chord. A total of 160 were built, including four that were

promotional vehicles for Pioneer electronics and came loaded with stereo gear where the rear seat had been. One oddity, car number 159, was actually assembled with a back seat.

For 1990–1991, a similar limited-edition Saleen was built, the SC. It had the SSC's power train plus a different intake manifold, but the car retained its rear seat. The intake was a joint venture between Saleen and Vortech Engineering, which was known for its centrifugal superchargers. The engine was now said to produce 304 horsepower at 5400 rpm, and the car was available in black, white, or red.

Sales peaked for Saleen in 1989, and as was the case with the high-end car market in general, interest waned shortly thereafter. There would be no SCs for '92, and the company was in poor health financially. Only ninety-eight cars were built in '91 (including nine SCs), and that figure plummeted to seventeen in '92.

There were the beginnings of a turnaround for Saleen in '93. Interest in the late-model Mustang was peaking, and Saleen was able to celebrate its tenth year by introducing the SA-10. Production was to be limited to ten vehicles; all would be black with yellow and silver accents on the hood and sides. Eight had all-black inte-

Above: Saleen sales more than doubled from 1987 to 1988. Although some coupes were produced from 1987 to 1990, most were hatchbacks or convertibles, like this 1988 model. **Above, inset:** Saleen Mustangs used a wide variety of wheels before 1983, with this basket-style being one of the busiest.

riors, and car number 3 had white seats. What made the SA-10 truly unusual was that it could be ordered with any engine part available in the Saleen Performance Parts catalog. This made for cars that were essentially unique under the hood but a hassle to produce. Eventually, nine were built, each with a base price of $36,995.

There was also an all-white Saleen custom-built for comedian Tim "Tool Man" Allen, star of the popular television show *Home Improvement*. Known as Casper, it had a fully worked engine, custom bodywork, tires, wheels, and more, and it garnered an incredible amount of attention.

FOX-4 SALEENS

While things were not necessarily looking their best for Saleen in the early 1990s, the company soon found itself the center of attention once again. The Ford faithful begged and pleaded for a 351-powered Mustang for 1994, but when the SN95 "Fox-4" car arrived, only two power plants were offered: the 3.8L V6 and the 5.0L V8.

For an independent like Saleen, opportunity not only knocked but kicked the whole damn door down. In 1994, Steve Saleen created the all-new S-351 Mustang, a styling tour de force that contained every hot piece of equipment Fox Mustang lovers dreamed of, including 18-inch (45.7cm) wheels and tires, a Tremec five-speed, and the all-conquering 351 engine producing 371 fuel-injected horsepower.

Saleen took the basic goodness of the new Mustang and stretched it to unprecedented levels. The engine was fortified with special large-valve Edelbrock cylinder heads, a trick intake manifold system, custom tube headers, and a unique calibration for its computer.

The cornerstones of the totally revamped suspension were the BFGoodrich Comp T/A tires (245/40ZR18s rear, 235/40ZR18s front) on 18- by 8.5-inch (45.7 by 21.5cm) five-spoke wheels (10-inch [25.4cm] wheels with Dunlop tires were an option). Naturally, the springs, shocks, and struts were of Saleen's own choosing, and Alcon four-piston calipers and monstrous rotors were

Above and inset: The 1989 SSC was the first Saleen to use an engine substantially different from what was available from Ford. They used ported cylinder heads, ceramic-coated headers, and other modifications, which increased the top speed to 156 mph (251kph), Saleen claimed.

standard as well. Form-fitting Recaro seats held you in place in high-g corners.

As for the body, a front air dam, a unique wing, and side skirts gave the Saleen a look of its own, a look far bolder than that of the standard Mustang. A hood with two indentations was optional.

For the truly adventurous, there was the Saleen SR (for Saleen Racer). Even larger rear brakes, drilled competition pedals, and a more race-oriented suspension were included, as were a large two-tiered wing on the decklid and a Vortech supercharger. The underhood windmill pumped up the ponies to 480, according to Saleen.

Saleen was hoping to move upward of four hundred or more cars in '94, but the complexity of the new build process was daunting. Ford drop-shipped V6 Mustangs to Saleen at its assembly facility in Irvine, California, where the cars were stripped down to their bare shells. Then in went the engines, suspensions, custom interiors, and so on. Production reached just forty-four S-351s in '95, along with two SR models.

For '95, S-351 production climbed to 126 (plus there were twelve SRs). The following year, Saleen got back to its roots. Taking advantage of the softness of the new GT while at the same time offering a car that was far easier to build, the company introduced the new S-281. Based on the 4.6L GT (281 cubic inches), it received Saleen bodywork and interiors, plus a race-bred suspension. Performance mods were limited to Saleen spark plug wires, a high-flow air filter, and 3.55:1 rear gears.

Though it handled great, it was not what you'd call a screamer in the acceleration department. Still, with a price of less than $30,000, the public snapped them up.

Below: When the new '94 Mustang hit the streets, many were disappointed that it lacked the powerful 351 engine. Saleen saw this as an opportunity and offered the S-351 with 371 or 480 horsepower, the latter with the aid of a supercharger. By 1998, all S-351s were supercharged.

Output reached 436, including a number of "Speedsters," gussied-up convertibles with light bars and tonneau covers that hid the rear seats.

The popularity of the S-281 took its toll on the S-351. Just twenty were assembled, and this author tested one. It covered the quarter mile (402.3m) in 13.62 seconds at 107.62 mph (173.1kph). With racing slicks, the time dipped to 12.40 at 109.98 mph (177kph). Top speed was 165 mph (265.4kph). Not bad for $42,000.

Muscle Mustangs & Fast Fords tested a supercharged S-351 in its June '96 issue, and this car proved even more fearsome, capable of 11.33-second quarter miles (402.3m) at 120 mph (193kph). It came at a high price—$52,079—but no other car could touch it for the money. *Road & Track* tested a similar vehicle, which topped out at 177 mph (284.7kph).

No production figures were available for '97 or '98, but the big news was that in '97, Saleen inked a deal with Budget to put a number of S-281s in its rental fleet. It also began production of the S-281 Cobra, won another racing championship, and competed at the fabled 24 Hours of Le Mans in France.

Below: Steve Saleen said the S-281 was close in concept to the original Saleen Mustangs. It had a basically stock engine (a 4.6 SOHC V8), but a modified suspension, interior, and bodywork. This is the Speedster version. **Opposite:** The S-281 hardtop offered Saleen exclusivity at a price that wasn't much higher than that of a Mustang Cobra. **Pages 102–103:** Saleen got back to its roots in 1996 with the S-281, which had all the looks and handling of the upmarket S-351, but with a virtually stock 4.6L (281 cubic-inch) engine. Pictured is a 1997 convertible.

THE TUNERS

Throughout the history of the Fox Mustang, there have always been people and companies that couldn't resist trying to improve the breed—to put their own stamp on it, so to speak. A $1-billion-a-year industry has sprung up for those trying to squeeze more performance from the 5-liter and, now, 4.6-liter engines. Today, there are superchargers, turbos, high-performance cylinder heads, cams, induction systems, and more, all available just a phone call away.

But many have made their marks building special-edition Mustangs that were not factory-certified like the ASC McLarens and Saleens. These companies would usually get cars from dealership stock and add their own bits and pieces until their version of the "ideal" ponycar emerged. Some offered little more than tape stripes and/or custom wheels. Others had complete suspensions, reworked engines, and/or celebrity endorsements.

The two most recognized tuners in the game at this writing are Steeda Autosports in Pompano Beach, Florida, and Kenny Brown Performance in Indianapolis, Indiana. Both are highly recognizable names in the Mustang aftermarket business and have incorporated what they've learned from racing into their street cars. Make no mistake, though: these are not uncivilized machines barely fit for human transportation. For the most part, both Steeda Autosports and Kenny Brown Performance offer highly optioned vehicles with superbly tuned suspensions and enough horsepower to satisfy even the most dedicated speed freaks.

Steeda was founded in 1988 by Steve Chichisola and Dario Orlando in southern Florida. The company has competed in both drag racing and road racing, and has applied the lessons it has learned at both venues to its street cars. The hallmark of the Steeda GT package over the years has been its compliant yet extremely competent suspensions. This company proved that through research and development, you could create a road-hugging Mustang that didn't beat its occupants silly.

Ironically, the original Steeda GTs were built on the LX 5-liter Mustang. They contained the obligatory wheel/tire upgrade—in this case 16- by 8-inch (40.6 by 20.3cm) Steeda Five Star rims and Bridgestone tires—plus body add-ons like a rear spoiler, a front air dam, and revised side skirts. Five-way adjustable Tokico shocks and struts were optional (ten years later, Steeda Mustangs still employ smooth-riding Tokicos), as were four-wheel disc brakes. Stiffer-than-stock lowering springs and urethane bushings were standard.

By 1990, the cars were pumping out 275 horsepower, according to Steeda, thanks to a revised intake manifold, an enlarged mass air meter, higher-ratio rocker arms, underdrive pulleys, and exhaust upgrades.

Come 1992, the Fifth Anniversary Steeda GT reflected much of the growth of the Mustang hobby and the automotive world. Standard were 17- by 8.5-inch (43.1 by 21.5cm) alloy rims with 245/40ZR17

Bridgestone tires. The Ford Motorsport GT-40 intake and GT-40 cast-iron heads comprised most of the free-breathing intake system—this was state-of-the-art hardware at the time. Steeda claimed 295 horsepower and a quarter-mile (402.3m) time of 13.3 seconds at 103 mph (165.7kph). Given the parts used, there's little reason to doubt these numbers.

These days, Orlando and company are concentrating on the ultimate 4.6L GT Mustangs. As with every Steeda Mustang, the suspensions get a complete makeover, and Vortech superchargers are optional. For '98, Steeda campaigned a specially prepared GT in Fun Ford Weekend competition. The 4.6 SOHC engine has fortified internals, Motorsport SVO cylinder heads, a trick intake, and a supercharger, and is said to make 450 rear-wheel horsepower.

Kenny Brown's Mustangs have one basic purpose: to handle like few other cars on the road while delivering the goods in a timely fashion without drawing too much attention. Oh, some Brown Mustangs have extroverted exteriors, but with the exception of custom wheels and tires (with a unique hood thrown in for good measure every once in a while), the Kenny Brown Mustangs are the Stealth Bombers of the Fox Ford set.

Brown was a veteran racer when he became the crew chief for Saleen's race team in 1987. Everything jelled and the team won its first SCCA championship that year. Soon after, Brown went out on his own, developing suspension goodies for his parts business. By 1989, he was producing his own brands of hellacious Mustangs, Lincoln Mark VIIs, Thunderbirds, and Tauruses. The Mustangs were known as the Super GT 250 and Super GT 275 (based on their horsepower ratings).

Each car received specific-rate springs, Koni adjustable gas shocks and struts, strut tower brace, heavy-duty lower chassis brace, urethane sway bar bushings, and urethane strut mount. Fittistar 16- by 7-

inch (40.6 by 17.7cm) wheels shod with Michelin 235/50ZR 16-inch (40.6cm) tires completed the chassis upgrades.

Acceleration enhancers came in the form of 3.27 or optional 3.55 gears, and a 65mm throttle body in the 250 and a balanced and blueprinted 5.0 with a 65mm TB in the 275.

Visually, the cars were hard to distinguish from stock Mustang GTs, which is just the way Brown wanted it. Only the wheels, a Super 250 or 275 windshield tint band, and subtle graphics differentiated them. A total of twenty cars were transformed in '89, including the first of Brown's "Outlaw" Mustangs.

His series of Outlaw Mustangs offered road course–ready suspensions, various engine output levels (a best of 335 in '90), and subtle good looks. The ultimate of his early Outlaw machines was the supercharged XS edition, which carried a Vortech blower, GT-40 intake, SVO four-bolt main block, and (!) a General Motors four-speed automatic transmission. Along with special seats and suspension upgrades, the XS lived up to its name.

Brown was still producing the Super GT (now LX), and the base package was the 250X, while the 290X replaced the 275. Like Saleen, Brown was hit hard by the recession of the early '90s. Just sixteen Mustangs were converted in '90 and only nine were transformed in '91. To add insult to injury, the lone '91 XS was totaled in a crash by a writer from *Car and Driver*. Nine more, including three Outlaw XS versions, were built in '92, and another six (three of them Outlaw XS cars) found homes in '93.

In 1994, Brown moved his company from Omaha, Nebraska, to world-famous Gasoline Alley, just blocks from the fabled Indianapolis Motor Speedway. The relo-

Below and inset: Kenny Brown was one of the driving forces behind Saleen's first SCCA championship. His Outlaw series of Mustangs delivered incredible handling and subtle good looks.

cation was much more complex and time-consuming than had been planned, and Brown could do little in the tuner car business. Most of his efforts concentrated on getting a new facility up and running and on keeping the production and sale of his line of high-performance parts moving. When this was accomplished, he focused his attention on a new car, the '95 320X Mustang. This potent performer depended on a GT-40-ized 5-liter engine (with aluminum heads) making 315 horsepower for motivation. But being a KB Mustang, the suspension would not go untreated. Brown's philosophy has always been to build from the ground up, with the car always having more cornering ability than horsepower. "The car's horsepower level dictates how we set up the rest of the car," explains Brown.

The 320X had Brown's level 4.1 Advanced Geometry Suspension, which means that—in addition to other unique features—it used adjustable Koni shocks and struts, low-deflection urethane bushings, and special springs. The 320X rode on OZ wheels and Bridgestone Expedia tires.

To commemorate the last of the 5-liter cars in '95, Brown teamed up with Callahan Ford, an Indianapolis-based Ford dealer, to produce the Super GT Series/Quarterhorse. It was quite a departure for Brown because the car came with a wild graphics package and a large front air dam. Among its other features was a T-handled Hurst shifter and the option of being built on either the GT or low-buck GTS model. Seven cars were built for Callahan Ford in '95, including one Cobra, one

Above: The Kenny Brown 320X derived its name from its modified 302 engine, which was said to produce 320 horsepower. It had Brown's 4.1 Advanced Geometry Suspension, which enabled it to outhandle cars costing twice as much.

Above: To commemorate the passing of the 5-liter engine in 1995, Kenny Brown and Callahan Ford (Indianapolis) created the Super GTS Callahan Quarterhorse. Based on the low-buck GTS Mustang, it had such retro touches as a T-handled Hurst shifter and side graphics reminiscent of the '68 Mustang GT. **Opposite:** The SAAC Mk II was available as a hatch or a convertible and, unlike the Mk I, came in red with white stripes.

GTS, and two six-cylinder cars that were dubbed the Pony Express package.

When the 4.6 Mustangs appeared in '96, Brown decided to concentrate on modifying the Cobra versions. This decision was based on the fact that his business for 4.6 GT parts was virtually nonexistent, while the Cobra parts continued to sell unabated. In '97 came the introduction of the C-4 Mustang (C for Cobra, 4 for the level of AGS suspension) and the C-4S (S for supercharged).

The C-4S was, by many accounts, the finest Kenny Brown supercar to date. It could outhandle a new Corvette, cover the quarter mile (402.3m) in 12.54 seconds on street tires, and stop like a race car, thanks to its enormous (and expensive) Brembo brakes. At more than $50,000, it most certainly was not inexpensive, but few new automobiles at any price could match or beat its performance.

BEST OF THE REST

There have been enough "special-edition" and "tuner" Mustangs built to fill an entire book, let alone a chapter in this one. But it would be remiss not to discuss some of the other memorable Stangs.

Most noteworthy was the SAAC Mk I. This car was built for the Shelby American Automobile Club and was sold only to club members in 1992. Marketed as EPA-certified automobiles, the cars started life as garden-variety Mustang GTs. Externally, the cars were white with blue "Shelby" stripes running from the hood, across the roof, and down the hatch. There were also GT350-style side stripes, but they ran just above the molding instead of along the rocker panels, like on the original Shelbys. The fog lights were removed from the front fascia, the "cheese grater" taillights had their louvers deleted, and unique side spats replaced the GT's factory

ground effects. Beautiful five-spoke 17-inch (43.1cm) wheels (7.5 inches [19cm] wide in front, 8 inches [20.3cm] wide in rear) wrapped in 245/45ZR Goodyears kept the car rolling.

Because Shelby club members no doubt demand a car that handles better than stock, higher-rate springs with a lower ride height and a strut tower brace were added. Four-wheel disc brakes with semimetallic pads were a huge improvement over stock.

Interior enhancements included repadded seats that offered more side bolstering, custom leather seat covers with white and blue inserts, a Hurst shifter, and a four-point roll bar.

The Mk I was rated at 295 horsepower, thanks to its GT-40 intake and iron cylinder heads, ceramic-coated headers, 65mm throttle body, and Dynomax cat-back exhaust system. SAAC was predicting 0- to 60-mph (96.5kph) times of 5.9 seconds, a blistering top speed of 151 mph (243kph), and 13.6-second quarter-mile (402.3m) times on street tires. The price for this road eater was $39,995.

The Mk I was successful enough that the Mk II was introduced later the same year, and this time a convertible was offered. Upgrades included adjustable shocks and struts, 3.27 rear gearing, and three color choices: white with blue stripes, red with white stripes, or black

with gold stripes (in honor of the '66 Shelby GT-350 Hertz rent-a-car). SAAC even arranged for insurance through Lloyd's of London. Again, production was limited to 250 units.

There were a host of other specials, including those offered by dealers and aftermarket parts manufacturers (such as the Dugan Viper and Mendhan Ford GT). One of the more curious was the Ronnie Sox Signature Series coupe from Shotgun Customs in Fayetteville, Georgia. Sox is a drag racing legend who raced Comets in the early 1960s and became a champion in the latter part of the decade in a slew of Plymouth Barracudas and Road Runners.

In 1990, Sox returned to the Ford camp, campaigning a replica of his '64 Comet in IHRA Pro Mod competition. To commemorate this (and to make some money), Shotgun introduced its Little Boss series. There were four iterations and either a four-cylinder engine or a 5.0 V8 was available. All had special side skirts, a different rear valence and wing, and a front spoiler, and they could be had in red, white, or blue paint.

The four-banger (the Littlest Boss) had all the body goodies plus suspension tweaks. Next up was the Little Boss 5-liter LX coupe, which was similar to the Littlest with the exception of the good engine. Four-wheel discs, 3.55 gears, and leather were optional.

The 5.0 SS added a Koni-enhanced suspension, with a traction-control damper, stiffer springs, and body braces. Four-wheel discs were standard on this version. At the top of the line was the Ultimate Boss, which added a Paxton supercharger to the equation.

Amazing thing about Mustangs. Since they debuted in 1964, there have been people who just couldn't leave it alone. Some of their work became little more than a blip on the radar screen of history; others, like the Shelbys and Saleens, actually made history. It is somehow comforting to know that as America's favorite ponycar gallops down the road into the twenty-first century, a hotter Mustang is probably just around the next curve.

Opposite: The 1992 SAAC Mk I was available only to members of the Shelby American Automobile Club. **Above:** A production 1998 Steeda Q, complete with supercharged 5.8-liter engine. **Following pages:** The crew at Steeda Autosports added horsepower and improved handling on its '98 Mustang GT conversions. These cars received a complete suspension makeover from Steeda's own line of high-performance parts. Added power came primarily from a Vortech supercharger.

Appendix

By the Numbers:
1993–1997 Cobra Production

The following is a breakdown of the production numbers and the color combinations of the 1993–1997 SVT Cobras and is presented courtesy of the SVT Cobra Owners Association's president, Robert Lyons.

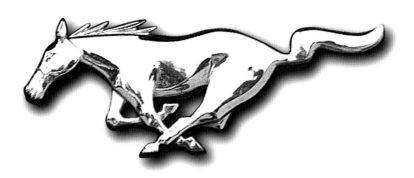

PRODUCTION BREAKDOWN BY MODEL		
Street	**Race**	**Total**
4,993	107	5,100

PRODUCTION BREAKDOWN BY COLOR			
Exterior Color	**Interior Color**	**Upholstery**	**Production**
Black	Black	Cloth	448
	Gray	Cloth	327
	Gray	Leather	1,079
			Total: 1,854 units
Red	Black	Cloth	362
	Gray	Cloth	522
	Gray	Leather	1,007
			Total: 1,891 units
Teal	Black	Cloth	185
	Gray	Cloth	368
	Gray	Leather	802
			Total: 1,355 units

1993

1994

PRODUCTION BREAKDOWN BY MODEL

Coupes	Convertibles	Total Production	
5,009 units	1,000 units	6,009 units	

PRODUCTION BREAKDOWN BY COLOR

Exterior color	Interior color	Upholstery	Production
Black	Black	Cloth	331
	Black	Leather	776
	Saddle	Cloth	130
	Saddle	Leather	558
			Total: 1,795 units
Red	Black	Cloth	333
	Black	Leather	625
	Saddle	Cloth	208
	Saddle	Leather	742
	Leather (convertible)	1,000	
			Total: 2,908 units
White	Black	Cloth	268
	Black	Leather	473
	Saddle	Cloth	123
	Saddle	Leather	442
			Total: 1306 units

1995

PRODUCTION BREAKDOWN BY MODEL

Coupe	Convertible	Total	
5,009	1,000	6,009	

PRODUCTION BREAKDOWN BY COLOR

Exterior Color	Interior Color	Upholstery	Production
Black	Black	Cloth	137
	Black	Leather	760
	Saddle	Cloth	55
	Saddle	Leather	1,484*
			Total: 1,795
Red	Black	Cloth	110
	Black	Leather	535
	Saddle	Cloth	85
	Saddle	Leather	717
			Total: 2,908
White	Black	Cloth	127
	Black	Leather	498
	Saddle	Cloth	316**
	Saddle	Leather	434
			Total: 1,306

* Total includes 1,003 black/saddle leather convertibles.   ** Total includes 250 white/saddle cloth R models.

BREAKDOWN BY MODEL

Coupe	Convertible	Total
7,496	2,509	10,005

COUPE PRODUCTION: BREAKDOWN BY COLOR

Exterior color	Interior color	Upholstery	Production
Black	Black	Cloth	13
	Black	Leather	1,376
	Saddle	Cloth	8
	Saddle	Leather	725
			Total: 2,122
Mystic	Black	Cloth	9
	Black	Leather	1,990
	Saddle	Cloth	0
	Saddle	Leather	0
			Total: 1,999
Red	Black	Cloth	16
	Black	Leather	926
	Saddle	Cloth	4
	Saddle	Leather	994
			Total: 1940
White	Black	Cloth	10
	Black	Leather	739
	Saddle	Cloth	10
	Saddle	Leather	676
			Total: 1,435

CONVERTIBLE PRODUCTION: BREAKDOWN BY COLOR

Exterior Color	Top Color	Interior Color	Upholstery	Production
Black	Black	Black	Cloth	2
	Black	Black	Leather	664
	Black	Sadddle	Leather	158
	Saddle	Black	Leather	5
	Saddle	Saddle	Cloth	1
	Saddle	Saddle	Leather	222
	White	Black	Leather	1
				Total: 1,058
Red	Black	Black	Cloth	2
	Black	Black	Leather	362
	Black	Saddle	Leather	36
	Saddle	Saddle	Cloth	1
	Saddle	Saddle	Leather	536
	White	Black	Cloth	1
	White	Black	Leather	13
	White	Saddle	Leather	11
				Total: 962
White	Black	Black	Leather	144
	Black	Saddle	Leather	11
	Saddle	Saddle	Cloth	1
	Saddle	Saddle	Leather	220
	White	Black	Cloth	2
	White	Black	Leather	59
	White	Saddle	Leather	57
				Total: 350

Breakdown by Model

Coupe	Convertible	Total
6,961	3,027	9,988

Coupe Production: Breakdown by Color

Exterior color	Interior color	Upholstery	Production
Black	Black	Cloth	43
	Black	Leather	1,641
	Saddle	Cloth	7
	Saddle	Leather	678
			Total: 2,369
Green	Black	Cloth	0
	Black	Leather	0
	Saddle	Cloth	27
	Saddle	Leather	1,028
			Total: 1,055
Red	Black	Cloth	39
	Black	Leather	1,131
	Saddle	Cloth	13
	Saddle	Leather	811
			Total: 1,994
White	Black	Cloth	20
	Black	Leather	817
	Saddle	Cloth	47
	Saddle	Leather	659
			Total: 1,543

Convertible Production: Breakdown by Color

Exterior Color	Top Color	Interior Color	Upholstery	Production
Black	Black	Black	Cloth	14
	Black	Black	Leather	840
	Black	Saddle	Cloth	2
	Black	Saddle	Leather	92
	Saddle	Black	Leather	12
	Saddle	Saddle	Leather	219
	White	Black	Leather	1
				Total: 1,180
Green	Saddle	Saddle	Cloth	4
	Saddle	Saddle	Leather	365
	White	Saddle	Leather	8
				Total: 377
Red	Black	Black	Cloth	6
	Black	Black	Leather	416
	Black	Saddle	Leather	15
	Saddle	Saddle	Cloth	7
	Saddle	Saddle	Leather	466
	White	Black	Leather	13
	White	Saddle	Leather	2
				Total: 910

1997

	CONVERTIBLE PRODUCTION: BREAKDOWN BY COLOR			
Exterior Color	Top Color	Interior Color	Upholstery	Production
White	Black	Black	Cloth	2
	Black	Black	Leather	190
	Black	Saddle	Cloth	1
	Black	Saddle	Leather	4
	Saddle	Black	Leather	7
	Saddle	Saddle	Cloth	4
	Saddle	Saddle	Leather	258
	White	Black	Leather	76
	White	Saddle	Cloth	3
				Total: 543

1997

Photo Credits

Automobile Quarterly Publications: pp. 8, 21 bottom, 38–39,

Kenny Brown Performance: p. 109, 110

Jim Campisano: ©Ford Motor Company: pp. 9, 76

Corbis-Bettmann: p. 49, 83

©Tom Corcoran: pp. 113, 114–115

FPG: ©Ford Motor Company: p. 77

©Jerry Heasley: emblem: pp. 5, 8, 10, 24, 44, 60, 76, 92, 114; pp. 2, 3, 12, 24–25, 26 both, 27 bottom, 30, 32, 33, 45 both, 52, 53, 57, 58 both, 62–63, 68 both, 69 top inset, 71, 72 both, 73, 74, 75, 85 both, 90, 98, 99 both, 100 bottom inset, 108 both, 111

Jerry Heasley Collection: pp. 16–17, 19, 22, 23, 34, 43, 46–47, 48, 55, 65 all, 66 both, 67, 84

©Ron Kimball: endpapers; pp. 51, 69, 94–95, 100 top, 101, 102, 103

©Dan Lyons: pp. 40, 41, 44, 59, 60–61, 96 bottom, 97, 104–105

©Doug Mitchell: pp. 15, 28–29

©Mike Mueller: pp. 6–7, 21 top inset, 77–78, 81 both, 82, 86–87, 91, 92–93, 90 top inset

Mike Mueller Collection: p. 80

Steeda: p. 89, 106 both, 107

UPI/Corbis-Bettmann: p. 13

©Nicky Wright: pp. 10–11, 54, 56, 112

Index